Critical Essays on Wordsworth
A New Approach

Critical Essays on Wordsworth
A New Approach

Anju Bala Agrawal

ABD PUBLISHERS
Jaipur ■ New Delhi

ABD PUBLISHERS

Regd. Off. "Bony Residency", Gate No. 2
Opp. Tilak Public School, Vishweswariya Nagar,
Gopalpura Road, Jaipur - 302018, India
Ph: 0141 - 2761280, Telefax: 2761381
Email: abdpublishersjpr@gmail.com

Delhi Office: 102, 1st Floor, Satyam House,
4327/3, Ansari Road, Darya Ganj,
New Delhi - 110002, India
Ph: 011-45652440

visit us: www.oxfordbookcompany.com

Published in India, 2024

ISBN : 9788183762175

Price : ₹ 1680/-

Typeset by Shivangi Computer, Jaipur

Printed and bound in India by Thomson Press Ltd.,
New Delhi

Dedicated to Respected
Guruji Shri Rasik Bihariji Joshi
whose blessings are always with me

Preface

No other poet in world literature has brought poetry so close to human heart as Wordsworth has done. He has revolutionized the art of poetry and has brought it near to human mind. He carries the conviction that poetry reveals the hidden truths of life. A poet is a seer and a prophet and poetry is a revelation, a magic incantation. Nature being central to his poetic art he looks at human being through its lens. Nature for him is not just lively rather it lives with greater force through a humanity which is so close to it. Among the romantics it was Wordsworth who was the most attracted by the beauty of nature. He liberated the poetic sensibility of his generation by revealing to it the world of English nature. The history of Wordsworth's romantic imagination lies embedded in vales, rills, rocks, stones and trees. He did see not only beauty in nature, but also a 'presence' which was some sort of spiritual being. On occasions, he also treated nature as a sort of teacher-moral teacher. He confessed that he grew up to be a poet, being informed by the beauty and terror of nature, and then he received moral teaching from nature. Wordsworth's poetry is such that it can be understood not with the brain alone but also with the sympathetic cooperation of the heart. Wordsworth is not just a Wordsworth in this age of globlization and liberalization. He has not just put a set of theory through his writings, but also has set before us the practice, which human beings should emulate. Wordsworth's wisdom will save the mankind at this critical juncture of time.

William Wordsworth, a collection of critical essays touches almost all the major aspects of the poet in a very simple, lucid and comprehensive way. The book, will certainly, prove to be very fruitful to all those students, research scholars and lovers of Wordsworth who want to be acquainted with the various aspects of Wordsworth's poetry and philosophy. The burgeoning ideas of Wordsworth, who knows, one day will compel us to go for a separate discipline like Wordsworth studies. Its interdisciplinary potential is enough, as it becomes a site where the branches of knowledge meet each other. Hope the present book on Wordsworth will act as a thought provoker for renewed interpretation of the poet. It will also promote more of research work.

I cannot close these prefatory remarks without expressing my gratitude to those who helped me in the preparation of this book. My indebtedness to previous scholars is greater than I can express and undoubtedly greater than I am aware of. I have quoted from them freely and have included in my essays what seem to be the best of their comments on a particular aspect of his poetry. To Professor De Selincourt, I owe most of all, as every student of Wordsworth must, because of the wealth and importance of the material, he has made available.

I deem it a priviledge and pleasure to place on record the valuable help and guidance that I received from various persons and institutions in my pursuit. Words fail to verbalize my sense of gratitude to Dr. Z. Hasan, Retired Reader, Department of English, K.R. (P.G.) College, Mathura who made my project easier than I imagined, more fun than I thought possible, and an education I didn't expect. It is only due to his constant help and scholarly guidance that I succeeded in completing my book. He has been a wonderful spring of support, encouragement and sustenance. I am indebted to several persons who have been very helpful during my studies-Dr. Preeti Johari, Principal, R.C.A. Girls' P.G. College, Mathura and Dr. Usha Garg, Head, Department of English of the same college. My thanks are due to the Librarian, Delhi University Library, Delhi and the Librarian, British Council Library New Delhi who procured for me the photocopies of several books and articles on Wordsworth. They helped me in tracing and consulting the material connected with my topic. I will be failing in my duty, if I do not express my sense of gratitude to the Librarian of Dr. B. R. Ambedkar University, Agra, the Librarian, R.C.A. Girls College, Mathura, the Librarian, A.M.U.Aligarh who helped me by promptly providing the books I needed.

I express my debt of gratitude to the members of my family whose unequivocal love and support, encouragement and co-operation helped me to complete my project. I am deeply beholden to my husband Shri Dinesh Agrawal. He allowed me full freedom to study so that I could devote myself whole heartedly to my studies. I would not have been able to complete my work without his help. Besides, my kids Bhavya and Virat, proved an extra impetus to me. Last but not the least a word of thanks also goes to the publisher of this book who published this book so nicely and promptly.

—Dr. Anju Bala Agrawal
Reader, Deptt. of English
R.C.A.Girls' P.G. College, Mathura

Contents

1

Nature and Man

Nature has always held an important place in English literature. It is another thing that in different ages it received different treatment. The stress may have shifted to something else, as is the case in the eighteenth century, but it has never been totally absent from English poetry. It is not a fact that writers of other countries have not painted Nature or have done it insincerely or perfunctorily, but the basic difference between the English writers and others is that the former have lived and breathed the natural atmosphere and have revelled with her. English poets, with regard to the treatment of Nature, have a place of their own.

Man has always been at the centre of creation but always fell from God's grace due to his own faults. Man and Nature are also part of the same cosmic design. Nature is crowded with animals and other lower creations but their great variety and ingenuity are testimonies of the Creator's wonderful power. During the Elizabethan age, the general outline of the medieval world picture survived. Nature in English poetry has sometimes taken the form of pastoralism. Pastoral poetry has also attracted our attention much and in the days of Shakespeare and Spenser this type of poetry had become very popular. Pastoral is a way out of "cares and perturbations" into:

> *Elysian regions where we are to meet with nothing but joy, and plenty and contentment; where every gale whispers pleasure and every shade promises repose.*[1]

In Spenser we find much of the abundance of Nature but in Shakespeare we find a more creative harmony and a spiritual discernment among English landscapes. Shakespeare was a genius. He created permanent spring for us and said that the enchanted ground lies very near to the inns and yards of the villages. The spell was still there in *The Sad Shepherd* of Johnson and the *Faithful Shepherdess of Fletcher* but it was not as forceful as it was in the hands of Shakespeare. William Browne of Tavistock wrote two books on *Britannia's Pastorals* by 1634. These long poems are wonderful in their simpler wooing of Nature.

Nature has always attracted attention playing upon the mysteries which have always surrounded her. In the earliest days Nature was thought to be a store house of evil forces to be feared and propitiated but during the Christian centuries, she had been consigned to the satanic order. Paganism and Stoic yearned for the Universe as the City of God. The Pauline and Augustinian theology opined that Nature was depraved and was groaning under divine malediction. The divine order and the grace of God was opposed to Nature. It was believed that the study of Nature was to repeat the original sin of Adam.

> *Francis Bacon was the first man to set in a different trend. He proved to the world that natural world was Promethean and not*

> *Mephistophelean. For practical purposes later fifteenth and sixteenth centuries may be taken as an epoch which showed the "rebirth of confidence in Nature."*[2]

We find the seventeenth century to be one, which produced writers who were bent upon changing people's attitude to Nature—from malevolent to benevolent one. Seventeenth century must be taken as the pioneer of a movement, which started the process of changing the very label, attached to Nature—she was not a foe but a friend to humanity and that the study of Nature was not anti-religious but a perfectly religious one. It is this attachment of religion with Nature that reached its zenith during the days of Wordsworth who developed his religion of Nature.

There have been innumerable writers who have found a number of messages from Nature. Henry Vaughan, a seventeenth century churchman, discovered God in all aspects of Nature. His poems remained ignored for two centuries. With full reverence for the modesty of Nature, Henry Vaughan records some of his institutions, which anticipate Blake and Wordsworth. Henry Vaughan is an illuminator of the humbler forms of Nature and country life and he has a greater appeal for the precursors of Romantic Revival. Thus the seventeenth century set the wheel rolling which came full circle during Romantic Age with some diversions.

The key word of eighteenth century poetry was 'Nature.' Nature was everywhere in religion, ethics, and philosophy and in politics but here, Nature is methodized, having nothing to do with the manifest nature of Wordsworth's landscapes. Nature has always been a controlling idea in Western thought but it was never as active as it was in the eighteenth century. It was an age of Spinoza, Shaftsbury, Newton, William Godwin, Joseph Priestley, David Hume and many others who emphasized Nature. Critics and poets were also continuously and habitually referring to Nature as their standards:

First follow Nature, and your judgement frame
By her just standard, which is still the same.

(Pope's Essay on Criticism)

We must copy Nature in order to be just and perfect. During the Middle Ages people held the idea of the controlling laws of nature, but the seventeenth and the eighteenth centuries found Nature as a liberating force. Nature during eighteenth century in literary world acquired two more meanings, i.e., reason and good sense. Basil Willey comments about this attitude:

"Nature for the poet is the idea, the form, the potentiality, which in history, and in fact, strive to realize themselves in refractory matter. Art completes what Nature leaves imperfect; Nature offers a brazen world—the poets only deliver a golden."[3]

Now the return was to new nature. The way was paved for a poetry which should devote itself to the study of Man in relation to Nature. During the time of Wordsworth it was commonly believed that Nature must form the main content of all poetry. In his book *Naturalism in English Poetry* Stopford Brooke says that: *"There are two great subjects of poetry. One of these (is) the natural world ... the other ... is human nature."*[4] The sociable eighteenth century gave a less important place to Nature, the meaning above mentioned. It held that proper study of mankind was Man, as such poetry describing Man was more appreciated. The eighteenth century attitude to Nature is clearer in James Beattie's views who say that human nature must come first. It never fails to arouse our interest:

Human affairs and human feeling are universally interesting. There are many who have no great relish for poetry that delineates only irrational or inanimate beings; but to that which exhibits the fortunes, the characters, and the conduct of men, there is hardly any person who does not listen with sympathy and delight ...

mere descriptions however beautiful and moral reflections, however just, become tiresome where our passions are not occasionally awakened by some event that concerns our fellow men. [5]

Like Beattie, most of the eighteenth century readers held that Nature was more interesting when it was involved with Man. Man gave to Nature its crowning interest and justified the extended description. The general and normal eighteenth century preference was for the natural scene which showed welcome sign to Man. The eighteenth century poet looked upon only those aspects or scenes of Nature which most pleasingly recalled to his mind the works of Man. Addison wrote in *The Spectator*:

We find the works of Nature still more pleasant the more they resemble those of art.

(Spectator No. 414)

Pope in *Windsor Forest* has also described woody landscape mirrored in the still waters of river Loddon. The scene appealed to Pope only because Nature was successfully mocking at Art. Man was the measure of all things in eighteenth century poetry. From the publication of Thomson's *Seasons*, Nature had started playing a more important part in poet's thoughts though he himself belonged to eighteenth century.

By the end of the eighteenth century, another change came over. The poetry of Blake, Cowper, Goldsmith, MacPherson, Chatterton, Gray and others foreshadowed the coming of a movement, which was to place Nature on a high pedestal. These poets were called the precursors of Romantic Revival. It is with Wordsworth that the revival of Romanticism began. Poets again returned to Nature and natural life. With the purpose of motivating the poets to compose poems along their lines and the people to love Nature and natural life,

Wordsworth and Coleridge brought about the publication of *Lyrical Ballads* in 1798. It set the movement in full swing. Now the poets and the people returned to Nature with a new outlook and renewed vigour. Thomson's *Seasons* is generally taken to be the point of Nature poetry but according to Peter Westland *The Nocturnal Reverie* by Lady Winchelsea should be regarded as the beginning of Nature poetry in English. Cowper had also opened windows to nature as she was in the woods and fields. Nature poets loved to think of man as a child of Nature communing with Her in complete obedience to Her laws and spirit.

The nineteenth century poets believed in the goodness of Nature. They believed that the order of the universe was purposive and harmonious and was benevolent towards man and other sensitive creatures. The precursors of the Romantic Revival, after setting the ball in motion, passed away. The rein now passed in the hands of poets like Wordsworth, Coleridge, Byron, Shelley and Keats. These poets were men with imagination and energy with firm determination to keep the fire ablaze. Now people saw the whole atmosphere vibrant with the spirit of Nature.

Henceforth I shall know
That Nature ne'er deserts the wise and pure,
No plot so narrow, be but Nature there,
No waste so vacant, but may well employ
Each faculty of sense, and keep the heart
Awake to Love and Beauty…

(*The Golden Book of Coleridge,* 76)

These five Romantic poets named above were the pillars of romantic poetry. They interpreted Nature in different ways according to their mental bent but the only string that bound them together was the spirit of Nature. Nature was at the centre of their poetry. She was the nucleus. She was the perennial source of their inspiration. She was a loving mother always ready to receive her prodigal sons back into her lap. The love and joy in Nature was so widespread that a man could not help but be happy in Her company. Wordsworth for the first time added a divine personality to Her. He derived pleasure, consolation, tranquil restoration and moral culture from the company of Nature. Coleridge believed Nature to be a storehouse of supernatural elements. Shelley passes beyond the visible shows of Nature to the larger cosmic operations in which she manifests Her power. In *Queen Mab* he says that the justice of Nature may be found in man's own heart. Keats sought beauty in every form of Nature. In fact, during the first half of the nineteenth century Nature suffused the mind and heart of the poet. They wanted a relief from the burdens of city life. Nature provided the relief by affording a calm and tranquil atmosphere. Wordsworth had changed the people's very way of life. John Stuart Mill, whose famous essay on Nature had given a severe jolt to the people's pre-conceived notions about the love and benevolence of Nature, too found solace in the poetry of Wordsworth. He read the poetry of Wordsworth that acted like a medicine to his ailing mind and heart:

> *"What made Wordsworth's poems a medicine for my state of mind, was that they expressed, not mere outward beauty, but states of feeling, under the excitement of beauty. They seemed to be the very culture of feelings, which I was in quest of. In them I seemed to draw from a source of inward joy, of sympathetic and imaginative pleasure, which could be shared in by all human beings. . . . From them I seemed to learn, what would be the perennial source of happiness, when all the greater evils of life shall have been removed."*[6]

Thus nature in the first half of the nineteenth century

was placed on a high pedestal. Benevolent nature was the main subject of poetry. In the second half of the century the pillars of Nature's empire shook by the onslaughts of materialism. The introduction of machines had disturbed the tranquility of Nature. Still nature and man was a favourite subject of poetry though the manner of presentation changed. Arnold spoke about the significance and importance of Nature's work. He took nature to be order of things. Tennyson was a landscape painter. Scientific inventions too contributed a great deal to the disfigurement of the face of Nature. Schopenhaur and J.S.Mill attacked the benevolent picture of Nature. These authors presented a completely new and reversed aspect of nature. The pre-conceived ideas were violently shaken but the old ones could not be completely uprooted. So the Victorian age became a battlefield of two opposing views of Nature. This continued for some time until Hardy came on the forefront. He showed a confirmed belief in the cruelty and malevolence of Nature for human beings. Hardy possessed the poetic sensibility with an inclination towards Nature and had a liking for Shelley and Keats. His preoccupation with Nature underwent stimulation after reading Mill and Darwin.

The twentieth century is a century of poetic diversity probably unequalled in history. The extremes of style and subject available to today's poets are further different than they have ever been before. Poetry today can be written on almost any subject. Modern poet finds inspiration from railway trains, tramcars, telephone, or other things of commonplace interest. One of the prominent characteristics of modern poetry is its passion for humanity, and its adoration of the life of the labourer, the miner, the cubman, the stoker and "the dust and scum of the earth". He perceived in the daily struggles of these people the same potentialities of a spiritual conflict that the older poets found in those of exalted rank. Wilfred Gibson is the best representative in modern English poetry of the poor toiling labourers, whose grim annals and dark horrors find an expression in his poetry. His well-known poem "The Machine" gives a pathetic but impressive picture of the dull, dead monotony of the life of mechanical labourers. Masefield expresses his creed in "Consecration". In this poem he becomes the spokesman of the workers and the toilers. He writes:

Not the rulers for me, but the ranker, the tramp of the road
The slave with the sack on his shoulder's pricked on with the goad,
The man with too weighty a burden, too weary a load.

Modern poets are lovers of Nature as well. Nature captivates the modern poet no less than the poets of other ages. In spite of the smoke and murkiness of the machine world of today modern poet feels a deep love and delight for Nature. It is not the spiritual or emotional life of Nature that fascinates the modern poet, but only the simple charm and poetry of her outward manifestation of flowers, birds, wind, countryside, etc. The modern poet writes of Nature with a rare freshness and vividness. Traces are visible of specialized love of certain region, as that of the south country by Robert Bridges. The sea has found its laureate in John Masefield. The poet today invests nature with his own moods. He fuses his subjective experiences with the objective realities of nature. His method is not photographic; it is impressionistic. He regards Nature as the highest excellence which Man has achieved through the gradual process of evolution.

Two of the most remarkable poets of the modern period combined tradition and experiment in their work. The Irish writer William Butler Yeats was the most traditional. In his romantic poetry, written before the turn of the century, he exploited ancient Irish traditions and then gradually developed a powerfully honest, profound and rich poetic idiom, at its maturity in "The Tower" (1928) and "The Winding Stair" (1933). T.S. Eliot was younger and he was born in the United States. He achieved more immediate acclaim with "The Waste Land" (1922). It was the most famous poem of the early part of the century. Through a mass of symbolic associations with legendary and historical events, Eliot expresses his despair the sterility of modern life. His movement towards religious faith displayed itself in "Four Quartets" (1943). His surprising combination of colloquial and literary diction, his fusing of antithetical moods and his startling, complex metaphorical juxtapositions relate him among English poets to John Donne. Eliot's style was intimately influenced by his study of such French poets as Jules Laforgue and Saint John Perse. Both Yeats and Eliot exercised enormous influence on modern poets. A third influence was that of Gerard Manley Hopkins, a Victorian poet whose work was not introduced to the world until 1918. The conflict between his Roman Catholicism and his sense of the beauty of this world and his complicated experiments in metrics and vocabulary attracted much attention.

Of the many poets stimulated to indignant verse by World War I, Siegfried Sassoon, Wilfred Owen and Robert Graves rank among the most lastingly important. Graves' ability to produce pure and classically perfect poetry kept his reputation strong long after World War II. The verse of Dame Edith Sitwell was first published during World War I. She communicated her disdain of commonplace propriety as much by the aristocratic individualism of her personal attitudes as by her poetry. She used extravagantly imaginative metaphors after the manner of the metaphysical poets. Conscious distortion of sense impressions somewhat as in modern painting was among her poetic devices. After World War II she wrote more compassionate and moving poetry as in "The Canticle of the Sun" (1949) and "The Outcasts" (1962).

The succeeding generation of poets, identified in the popular consciousness with the depression and social upheaval of the 1930s, made use at first of so much private or esoteric symbolism as to render the poetry barely intelligible to any but a small coterie of readers. The best known of these – W.H. Auden, Stephen Spender and C. Day Lewis – filled their earlier poetry with political and ideological discussion and with expressions of horror at bourgeois society and nascent totalitarianism. W.H. Auden's Nature poetry is unique in the amazing variety of ways in which he works. Here it may be noted that Auden's concern is more for man than for Nature. His Nature poems are primarily poems about men. In his poetry Nature is merely a background to human activity. As he says: "To me art's subject is the human clay / And landscape but the background to a torso". Auden's poetry became more reflective in "The Double Man" (1941) and later, "City without Walls" (1969). So, too, Day Lewis moved from "The Magnetic Mountain" (1935) to a more personal lyricism in "World Above All" (1943). His "Poetic Image" (1947) was a prose exposition of the modern poetic ideal. The position of poet laureate, held by Day Lewis from 1968 to 1972, subsequently passed to Sir John Betjeman popular for his nostalgic humour. A militant preservationist, he aimed his poetic wit at those who, in the name of progress, threatened to despoil the English countryside.

Experimentalism continued in the exuberantly metaphorical poetry of the Welsh writer Dylan Thomas, whose almost mystical love of life and understanding of death were expressed in some of the most beautiful verse of the middle of the century. After Thomas' death in 1953, a new generation of British poets emerged, some influenced by him and some reacting against his influence. Among the leading poets of that generation were D.J.Enright, Philip Larkin, John Wain, Thom Gunn, and Ted Hughes. Although they had different styles, these poets constituted what became known as The Movement and sought to appeal to the common reader with a non-sentimental poetry of everyday, written in colloquial language. Larkin (*Collected Poems*, 1988) often wrote of deprivation and absence. Hughes, whose poetry is noted for its depiction of the savagery of life, became one of England's most significant poets and was made poet laureate in 1984 after the death of Betjeman. Poet and critic Andrew Motion was named poet laureate in 1999, after Ted Hughes' death.

Prominent British poets of the late 20th century included Craig Raine, Wendy Cope, James Fenton and Seamus Heaney. Raine's early collection, *A Martian Sends a Postcard Home* (1979), brings a fresh viewpoint to many topics. Wendy Cope's witty insights appear in *Making Cocoa for Kingsley Amis* (1986). Fenton's collection *Out of Danger*_(1994) covers love, war and the political violence he encountered as a war correspondent in south-east Asia. Heaney, from Northern Ireland, won the 1995 Nobel Prize in Literature. His poetry appears simple in its language and flow, its structure and references are often complex. All poets of twentieth century have dealt with Nature and Man in some way or the other, though their manner of depiction is different from earlier ages. In fact, literatures of all the languages of the world find Nature and Man as their favourite theme.

References

1. Blunden, E., *Nature in English Poetry,* The Hogarth Press, London, 1949, p. 89.
2. Willey, B., *The Seventeenth Century Background,* Chatto and Windus, London, 1962, p. 33.
3. Willey, B., *The Eighteenth Century Background,* Chatto and Windus, p. 27.

4. Brooke, Stopford, *Naturalism in English Poetry*, 1920, p. 19, quoted in *A Preface to Eighteenth Century Poetry* by Sutherland, J., Oxford Paperback (O.U.P.) 1963, p. 111.

5. Beattie, James, *Essays on Poetry and Music*, 1776, p. 373, quoted in *A Preface to Eighteenth Century Poetry*, p. 111.

6. Quoted in *Wordsworth's Fame*—by House, H., an Essay in *English Critical Essays* (Twentieth Century, II Series) (ed.) Derek Hudson, O.U.P. London, 1958, p. 254.

2

Life and Writings

William Wordsworth is a major poet in English literature. He is probably the greatest poet of Nature in the world. He was a prolific writer and composed a large number of poems. In order to know about Wordsworth, we need not go anywhere as *The Prelude* itself is the record of his life. It is a source of positive information about the life and work of Wordsworth. Wordsworth was born in 1770 at Cockermouth in Cumberland in the north of that lake country which he loved so well. He was the second child of a fairly thriving attorney-at-law, John Wordsworth. His mother Anne was the only daughter of William Cookson, a well-to-do mercer at Penrith. As a child his life was not particularly distinguished. He was "of a soft, moody and violent" temper; therefore, his mother was always worried about him. He had pleasant hours with his brothers and sister till he was taken to his mother's family at Penrith after the death of his mother at the age of eight. His grandparents often treated the little ones rather harshly. He was deprived of the blessings of a happy home. His father's death, at the age of thirteen, was the second shock for the adolescent.

He was sent to Hawkshead Grammar School and it was not a happy place for him. He had no intellectual company and found solace in his precious books and in personal freedom from restraint. He read all Fielding's works, *Don Quixote, Gil Blas, Gulliver's Travels, The Tale of a Tub*, etc. "However, it was not from books, but from his early associations with Nature that he was to find his real inspiration."[1] He found great delight in games and in rambles about hills and lakes. He became familiar with English mountain scenery and the subduing spirit of its beauty touched his earliest life. He himself tells us:

Haunting me thus among my boyish sports
On caves and trees, upon the woods and hills
Impressed upon all forms the characters
Of danger or desire;

(*The Prelude I*, 469-72)

He went in 1787 to St. John's College, Cambridge, where he found little to interest him. He remained there till the beginning of 1791. He could not show any deep passion for intellectual and literary pursuits. At first, he was attracted by the sloth and wildness of the student's life; but soon he was repelled by it. That he did not like the university atmosphere is evident from the following lines that he wrote in *The Prelude*:

Of college labours, of the Lecture's room,
All studded round, as thick as chairs could stand,
With loyal students, faithful to their books,
Half-and-half idlers, hardy recusants,
And honest dunces; of important days,

Examinations, when the Man was weigh'd
As in the balance—of excessive hopes,
Trembling withal, and commendable fears,
Small jealousies and triumphs good or bad.

(*The Prelude III*, 64-72)

Wordsworth spent his first summer vacation at Hawkshead. He felt a new sympathy for the old dame in whose house he still lodged. Here "after a night spent in dancing, he was deeply moved by a splendid sunrise. He felt that he was henceforth a 'dedicated spirit'." Speaking of this experience, Wordsworth says:

Ah! Need I say, dear friend! that to the brim
My heart was full: I made no vows, but vows
Were then made for me; bond unknown to me
Was given, that I should be, else sinning greatly.
A dedicated spirit.

(*The Prelude IV*, 333-37)

His second long vacation was passed in touring through Dovedale to Penrith and it brought him a further gain in human affections. He rambled with his sister Dorothy and her friend Mary Hutchinson, who had been his school fellow at Penrith, and who later became his wife.

In his third long vacation, he undertook a "pedestrian tour" through France and Switzerland. It seems probable that Wordsworth and his friend Robert Jones were actually the first undergraduates who ever spent their summer in this way. "Wordsworth and his friends encountered on this tour many a stirring symbol of expectancy that was running through the nations of Europe."[2] Wordsworth heartily enjoyed this expedition. It may be noted here that during this tour, Wordsworth landed at Calais, "on the very eye of that great federal day", when the trees of liberty were planted all over

France. The two friends returned to Cambridge in October 1790. Wordsworth took his B.A. degree on January 27th, 1791 and left Cambridge with no fixed intentions for his future career.

Meanwhile financial stringency was beginning to make life difficult for him. His uncle now put pressure to enter a profession but he could not even choose a profession. The army, the law, the church were all thought about and rejected in turn. He felt solitary and morose. Perhaps he couldn't recognize the truth that he was suffering from the "growing pains" of a poet. After leaving Cambridge, he settled in London, "pitching a vagrant tent among the unfenced regions of society". His patrimony had been spent on his education and he was without a profession or any qualifications for a profession. He was worried about his future, though these dark facts find no expression in *The Prelude.*

In November 1791, he set out for France for a second time as he had a desire to improve his knowledge of French. There he remained, namely at Orleans and Blois till December 1792. His general enthusiasm for the Revolution was now quickened by a closer study of its purposes and by personal contact with some of its opponents and some of its more idealistic supporters. Wordsworth was confirmed in his belief that the Revolution was a natural expression towards human liberty. Meanwhile events in France moved rapidly as the dethronement of Louis XVI, the massacres by the Jacobins, etc., in October came to Paris but his revolutionary faith was still undiminished by the element of terror in recent events. At Orleans, he had met Marie Anne Vallon, the daughter of a well established Royalist family of Blois. Their attachment was immediate and passionate and in December 1792, a daughter named Caroline was born. The years that immediately followed his return to England were among the unhappy in his life. In

January 1793, Louis XVI was executed and by February, England was at war with France. This armed opposition of England came as the deepest shock for Wordsworth's moral nature as he describes in *The Prelude X:*

> *Oh, pity and shame! With those confederate*
> *Powers !*
> *Not in my single self alone I found,*
> *But in the minds of all ingenuous youth,*
> *Change and subversion from that hour.*
>
> (*The Prelude*, 264-67)

Wordsworth could not forget Annette as the "Dear child, dear Girl" of the sonnet "It is a beauteous evening, calm and free", composed on Calais Beach, in 1802, describes. Wordsworth's early life with French affairs, early passion and later business relations with Annette remained a secret of literary history for long and were revealed only a century ago by George McLean Harper in his work *William Wordsworth: His Life, Works & Influences* (1916). Wordsworth's activities in France were not confined to attempts to make himself a French citizen. Now he began to feel the importance of poetry in his life.

When the French Revolution passed into terror, Wordsworth lost his trust in social reform. "He turned to abstract meditation on man and society. Godwin's *Political Justice* became a kind of Bible that comforted his distress. But the abstract anarchistic doctrine of Godwin was utterly useless to a creative poet."[3] Its influence can be seen on his dramatic work *The Borderers*. Wordsworth had to see much rise and fall in his life. The war between England and France not only saved him from an unsuitable alliance but also from the guillotine in 1793.

In 1795, all his resources seemed exhausted. It became

difficult to maintain the life of a poet. Salvation dropped from the clouds in the form of a legacy of 900 pounds, left for him by a young friend who believed that immediate relief might help him to live for poetry. To Wordsworth it was a boon. He put an end to his wandering life and settled down with his sister Dorothy at Racedown in Dorsetshire. Dorothy redeemed him from the state of lethargic aimlessness. "She revealed to him the true bent of Nature, and discovered to him his true powers. She led him back to the healing solitude of Nature, where alone, as she justly perceived, his mind could find a fit environment, and his powers could ripen into greatness."[4]

In the summer of 1797, he moved from Racedown to Alfoxden because Coleridge was living at Nether Stowey in Somersetshire quite near to Alfoxden. Now the conversation between the two great poets was possible and now began a friendship which for its mutual influence has no parallel in English Literature. It is difficult to say with any exactness how for they influenced each other, but it is certain that they had a highly stimulating effect upon each other. Due to the failure of French Revolution to maintain high ideals, Wordsworth suffered a moral crisis. Now, under the restorative influence of Nature and the affection and encouragement of Dorothy and Coleridge, he regained his mental peace. He felt so self-assured that he planned to write a great philosophical poem *The Recluse,* but it was never completed; it exists in fragments that were to make up the whole—the first book of *The Recluse, The Prelude* and *The Excursion.*

This was the time when his creative power and imagination were at their best. In fact, these were the most fruitful years of Wordsworth's life. In 1798 was published the *Lyrical Ballads,* to which Coleridge contributed "The Ancient

Mariner". It was an epoch making production but it was hardly recognized at that time. It opened up a new horizon for English poetry. *The Prelude* (published in 1850), "Ode to Duty", and "Immortality Ode", *The Excursion* and many other poems and sonnets belong to the period of 1797-1814.

In the autumn of 1798, Wordsworth along with his sister Dorothy and Coleridge went to Germany. Wordsworth liked to stay at Goslar, whereas Coleridge moved to Ratzeburg. On account of severe cold, Wordsworth remained confined to his lodgings and devoted his time to learning German language from books and dictionaries. Here Wordsworth wrote some of his best poems like "Ruth", "Nutting", "The Poet's Epitaph", and the "Lucy Poems". Here it was that he planned and began *The Prelude*. "Coleridge's absence, the isolation of his daily life in the little German city, the presence of Dorothy, herself a link with his earliest days, lack of books and outside interests, all alike combined to make his mind a more than usually clear mirror of his own experience. In some such manner, we may conclude, *The Prelude* began to be written."[5] German philosophy and literature had very little effect on him so he decided to settle down among his native mountains. In Dec. 1799, Wordsworth and Dorothy returned to their beloved Lake country and settled at Dove Cottage, Grasmere.

In 1802, he married his cousin, Mary Hutchinson, who proved to be a devoted wife and companion to Wordsworth. Wordsworth was lucky in having a wife who if not possessed of the remarkable accomplishments and insight into the beauties of Nature as possessed by Dorothy, had yet qualities which were calculated to make her home happy. The poem, "She was a Phantom of Delight", is a faithful description of her:

A countenance in which did meet
Sweet records, promises as sweet;

A creature not too bright or good
For human nature's daily food;
For transient sorrows, simple wiles,
Praise, blame, love, kisses tears and smiles.

(She Was a Phantom of Delight, 15-20)

Next year, he went on a visit to Scotland, where he met Scott. He shifted to Rydal Mount in 1813 to live there for the rest of life. "The great work of his early and middle years was now over, and Wordsworth slowly settled into the role of patriotic, conservative public man, abandoning the radical politics and idealism of his youth."[6] In the same year, he was appointed Distributor of Stamps for his district. The income was a welcome addition to the poor resources of the poet.

Now his fame was growing and his work started finding favour. He wandered through European countries such as Holland, Belgium, France, Italy, Switzerland, Scotland, etc. He was spending his life in calm retirement among the scenes he most dearly loved. But he suffered a number of misfortunes as well. Illness of Dorothy and death of some near and dear persons cast a veil of gloom on the poet's decaying physical powers. In 1842 he was placed on the Civil Pension List and on the death of Robert Southey in 1843, he succeeded to the Poet-Laureateship. The most important poem of this period is "Laodameia". In 1859, he died peacefully, with a whole nation, now at last conscious of his greatness, mourning his loss. His body was buried, as he had wished in Grasmere churchyard.

Wordsworth's Writings

Wordsworth was a voluminous writer. His poetic span covers a period of more than sixty years. So far as the bulk of poetry is concerned, few can challenge comparison with him. He continued to write till the very end of his days. His best poetry was produced during the decade 1797-1807. It has been customary to divide Wordsworth's poetic career into different parts, accordingly as his powers were at their height or declining, or totally wanting. Herbert Read divides his period of creative activity into the following four parts:

The Early Period

This period is before 1791. The best known poems of the period are (1) the "Descriptive Sketches" and (2) "Evening Walk".

The Period of Gloom

The period of guilt and remorse was from 1792 to 1797. His feeling of remorse and his gloom find expression in the unsuccessful tragedy, *The Borderers,* "Guilt and Sorrow" and "The Ruined Cottage". The last mentioned poem was later incorporated into *The Excursion.*

The Glorious Decade

The glorious decade is from 1797 to 1807, the decade in which the poet's powers were at their zenith and in which he produced his best works.

1. *The Lyrical Ballads* (1798) contained many admirable pieces, such as "Lines Written in Early Spring", "Michael", Fountain, etc., and ending with the "Lines Written above Tintern Abbey".

2. "Peter Bell" .

3. "Lucy Poems", "Nutting" and "Ruth".

4. *The Prelude,* or the account of the growth of a poet's mind, commenced in 1799 and completed in 1805, though published only after his death in 1850. It runs

into fourteen books and has universal significance and appeal.

5. "The Immortality Ode" begun in 1802 on the eve of his happy marriage and completed in 1805.

6. The Two Volumes of 1807 started in 1804. The great poems of this period include "Ode to Duty", "Highland Girl", "Solitary Reaper", "Affliction of Margret", "Happy Warrior", "Resolution and Independence", "Peele Castle", "To the Cuckoo", "My Heart Leaps up", "I Wandered Lonely as a Cloud", etc.

7. *The Excursion,* began about the year 1802 and published in 1814. It runs into nine books.

8. *The Sonnets.* Wordsworth was inspired to write sonnets on hearing the sonnets of Milton read out to him in 1801. He continued to write sonnets up to the end of his days and has left behind his more than 500 pieces. The best of his sonnets are: "Sonnet on the Sonnet", "Milton", "Composed upon Westminister Bridge", "The World is too much with Us", and the series on "The River Duddon".

The Period of Decline

This period is from 1808 to 1850. The old fire was gone but Wordsworth continued to write. To this period belong such pieces as: "Laodameia", "Ecclesiastical Sketches", "Sonnet on the Punishment of Death", "Lines Written on the Death of Charles Lamb, "Effusion on the Death of James Hogg", etc.

Literary Criticism

His "Preface to *The Lyrical Ballads* (1802), revised and enlarged for subsequent editions, is a critical document of abiding significance.

Such is the poetic career of one of the greatest poets of England, one to whom Matthew Arnold assigns a place next only to Shakespeare and Milton.

References

1. Compton, Rickett: *A History of English Literature*, London, Thomson Nelson & Sons Ltd., 1956, p. 307.
2. Myers, F.W.H., *Wordsworth*, London, Macmillan &Co. Ltd., p. 13.
3. Sampson, George, *The Concise Cambridge History of English Literature*, London, Cambridge University Press, 1970, p. 477.
4. Dawson, W.J., *The Makers of Modern English*, Meerut, Shalabh Book House, 1985, p. 105.
5. Moorman, Mary, *William Wordsworth—A Biography: The Early Years 1770-1803*, London, Oxford University Press, 1957, p. 421-22.

3
Influences

Every writer is influenced by a number of factors. So was William Wordsworth. No doubt, he had genius, but the influence of a number of persons, including some of his friends, and contemporary events on him cannot be ruled out. He was considerably influenced by the following factors:

Political Influences

Some of the noblest verses of Wordsworth and all his majestic prose were inspired by political passion. He holds the French Revolution which broke out with the breaking down of the Bastille and he claims:

Bliss was it in that dawn to be alive,
But to be young was very heaven!

("French Revolution", 4-5)

A holiday journey to France and Switzerland in 1790 provided the material for "Descriptive Sketches" written in couplets in the manner of the eighteenth century topography and written well enough but without much sign of Wordsworth's individual power. More important was the political atmosphere and it is from now onwards that political and public events begin to play a major part in his development.

The fundamental fact about Wordsworth's politics is that he was a trueborn English man. His roots were struck deep in English soil. In his youth he was an ardent admirer of English politics. His expressions were explicit and remarkable to show his admiration of parliamentary democracy. At Cambridge, Wordsworth threw himself forcefully into the course of freedom and "sang his lofty gratulation unawed amid a slavish band". Utilitarian ethics and political freedom were important concerns of Wordsworth's life. Wordsworth's hopes, hopes in the people rather than in their leaders, look on a new lease of life, centered only by bitter scorn and indignation against the English political leaders who insisted on fighting what seemed the inevitable course of nature and justice. He writes in *The Prelude:*

The earthquake is not satisfied at once;
And in this way I wrought upon myself,
Until I seemed to hear a voice that cried,
To the whole city, 'sleep no more'.

(*The Prelude* X, 84-87)

But from the time that Britain opposed the liberties of France with open wars; a change began to take place, not only in Wordsworth's opinions but in his whole attitude to the world. In 1798, his ideal of France was finally shattered by the encroachment of Switzerland. Coleridge made haste to renounce Wordsworth's Republicanism in his "Ode to France". But he didn't listen, didn't react but turned away from politics altogether to devote himself to poetry. His ideals had changed. Joy in common objects was still his goal, but he no longer tried to make for it along the path of political reform.

In August 1802, after the peace of Ameens, he spent a month at Calais with Annette and their daughter. Now Wordsworth started taking a little interest in foreign politics. In 1803, war broke out again. Political problems occupied Wordsworth more and the legal and dogmatic element of his nature became more eminent in his treatment of them as his poetic activity declined. The disposition to "touch and handle little truth, which had marked the temporary obscuration of his imagination returned upon him in his decay".[1]

Under the influence of Beaupuy, Wordsworth felt himself vicariously a patriot and a man of action and he contracts his aspect of abstract political discussion in academic groves with the sense of participation in a great historical process that his present situation gave him. His several sonnets of the period between 1800 and 1807 bear testimony to his change. It means the sonnets which he classed as political sonnets and included among poems "Dedicated to National Independence and Liberty". Almost the first and best is the famous sonnet "On the Extinction of the Venetian Republic":

Once did She hold the gorgeous east in fee;
And was the safeguard of the west: the worth
Of Venice did not fall below her birth,
Venice, the eldest Child of Liberty. (1-4)

His old interest in Spain also revived to some extent. Whatever the changes of his political creed, there was no doubt Wordsworth loved his fellowmen with an extreme intensity. Whatever Milton lacked, Wordsworth supplied in a supreme measure. Though accidents had cast him among the adversaries yet by nature he was very liberal.

French Revolution

Almost all the Romantic poets were influenced by this event. It had its impact on Wordsworth's outlook on life, nature and society. The ideals of French Revolution did not come to Wordsworth as a matter of surprise for he had passed through societies where these ideals in one form or the other already existed. Wordsworth's knowledge of the French Revolution came from the writings of Burke, Paine and other detractors and vindicators. He needed an objective chronicle of the Revolution, which might show whence the organs of public power had sprung. Wordsworth was a supporter of Revolution, a penniless Englishman with no certain means of livelihood. Wordsworth describes the terror that started in France. In *The Prelude,* he describes the desolating effect. It had on all who had placed their ideal hopes in the Revolution. In *The Prelude,* Wordsworth explains how the Revolution presented itself to his thinking and feeling as the most natural thing in the world. At first, it found him almost indifferent:

I stood 'mid those concussions, unconcerned,
Tranquil almost, and careless as a flower
Glassed in a greenhouse, or a parlour shrub
That spreads its leaves in unmolested peace,
While every bush and tree, the country through,
Is shaking to the roots: indifference this
Which may seem strange;

(*The Prelude* IX, 86-92)

Wordsworth's first sympathies with the Revolution were merely sentimental. He settled first at Blois, then at Orleans, moving first in the kind of respectable society where the turmoil of the times was not mentioned. Becoming bored with this company, he began to mix with the common world. He conceives that through his life, the whole trend of his mind has been in direction of nature and freedom and just upon this account the events of Revolution; as he beheld them developing in France, so far from shaking mind or habit in him:

Seemed nothing out of nature's certain course but,
A gift that was come rather late than soon.

(*The Prelude* IX, 247-48)

Wordsworth's ignorance of the actual progress of the Revolution hindered his appreciation of the events, he witnessed at first hand. When Wordsworth made a walking tour to Switzerland, he had to pass through France both ways. But that spectacle of the revolutionaries made little impact on his sensibilities at first. During that tour, he collected material for "Descriptive Sketches".

At the time of his second visit to France, he came closer to Revolution. He got the opportunities of meeting and mixing with the patriots and revolutionaries and knew their feelings and thoughts more closely. One such revolutionary was Beaupuy. Before Wordsworth's intimacy with Beaupuy, his interest in the Revolution was largely sentimental but his friendship with the republican officer Beaupuy brought a deeper concern in the Revolution. Wordsworth writes:

Among that band of officers was one
Already hinted at, of other mould
A patriot, I thence rejected by the rest
And with an oriental loathing spurned,
As of a different caste.

(*The Prelude* IX, 288-92)

Wordsworth's heart was all the more grieved when England joined war. He was so sad that he never went to the churches at the time of offering prayer in churches for England's victory. But at the same time, he was shocked to see France as the destroyer of all that was grand and noble. Wordsworth expresses his mental agony. To quote:

Most melancholy at the time, O Friend
Were my day-thoughts,-my nights were miserable;
Through months, through years, long after the last beat
Of these atrocities, the hour of sleep
To me came rarely charged with natural gifts,
Such ghastly visions had I of despair
And tyranny, and implements of death;

(*The Prelude* X, 397-403)

Wordsworth was so shocked that he tried to find solace in abstract political theories of Godwin. In order to cast off the gloom and despair, he sought refuge in the beneficent Nature and began to find a serene confidence in human nature as well.

Beaupuy

He was a Republican captain, a man of intellect and of humanitarian ideal, who later became Wordsworth's greatest friend. To quote:

Oft in solitude
With him did I discourse about the end
Of civil government, and its wiser forms;
Of ancient loyalty, and chartered rights,
Custom and habit, novelty and change;
Of self respect, and virtue in the few

For patrimonial honour set apart,
And ignorance in the labouring multitude.

(*The Prelude* IX, 321-28)

Wordsworth and Beaupuy, a republican captain walked frequently along the Loire, or through forest tracts where Wordsworth sometimes forgot the present in imaginative re-creation of scenes in Aristo or Tasso or Spenser. Beaupuy was honourable, scholarly, gentle and courteous to all.

Godwin

Godwin was an English political philosopher and novelist, who, as a person and as a writer exerted a profound influence on the younger authors of his time. His *Political Justice* was accounted in its time an immortal book. It exercised a powerful influence upon Wordsworth. Hazlitt in his Essay "Spirit of Age" writes: "No work in our time gave such a blow to the philosophical mind of the country as the celebrated Enquiry concerning *Political Justice.*

Wordsworth remained under the influence of Godwinism from 1793 to 1797. It has two main divisions. Of these, the first and longest lies between the spring of 1793 and the summer of 1795. It may be called the epoch of semi-Godwinism. Wordsworth describes himself as having, during this period lent but a careless ear to the pretensions of Godwin, which were, however, "sedulously urged" upon him.

In these years the influence of Godwin upon Wordsworth was deep but not sufficiently deep to exclude other influences and hopes. Only after August 1793, Wordsworth's views of inter connection between Man and Nature comes to him with the raucous ring of Godwinism. It was at this time that he began to compose "Guilt and Sorrow". This poem is distinctively Godwinian. Actually the plots of "Guilt and Sorrow" and *The Borderers* are derived from Godwin's *Caleb Williams*. The period of fuller Godwinism may be dated in July 1795 and ends without any specification in *Lyrical Ballads*. Coleridge's "France an Ode" is a valuable commentary upon Wordsworth's revolutionary Godwinian period.

Throughout *The Prelude*, Godwin is nowhere mentioned by name. There are several lines, which indicate Godwin's influence.

Meantime,
As from the first, wild theories were afloat
To whose pretensions, sedulously urged,
I had but lent a careless ear, assured
That time was ready to set all things right.

(*The Prelude* XI, 188-92)

The extreme of Godwinian influence can be seen in these lines:

With a resolute mastery shaking off
Infirmities of nature, time and place
Build social upon personal liberty;
Which, to the blind restraints of general laws
Superior, magisterially adopts
One guide, the light of circumstances, flashed
Upon an independent intellect.

(*The Prelude* XI, 238-44)

Dorothy

Wordsworth and Dorothy were intimately attached to each other. After his wandering life, Wordsworth came to settle with Dorothy at Racedown in 1795. Dorothy was a direct link with Wordsworth's childhood. She shared joys as well as his sorrows. Wordsworth says about Dorothy:

Then it was-
Thanks to the bounteous Giver of all goods-
That the beloved sister in whose sight
Those days were passed, now speaking in a voice
Of sudden admonition—like a brook
* * *
She whispered still that brightness would return;
She, in the midst of all, preserved me still.

(*The Prelude* XI, 333-48)

The two had an intimate relationship. Her fine and beautiful regard for common things gave a healthy tone to all his perception and helped to transform mere observation "The tyranny of the eye into imaginative vision". Dorothy brought him back to life of all the senses after the unjust behaviour of a life of abstract thought. She not only reminded him of his vocation on earth, but she also softened a certain authority that was present in him, and awakened his heart to a "mild influence". How complete was the recovery of the poet under the humanizing and tranquilizing impact of beloved sister is seen in the *Biographia Literaria*. Wordsworth says that Dorothy did a lot for him. To quote,

The blessing of my later years
Was with me when a boy
She gave me eyes, she gave me ears;
And humble cares and delicate fears.

(The Sparrow's Nest)

"Three Years She Grew" was composed in the Harz Forest and this might be regarded presumptive evidence that its Lucy is Dorothy.

And vital feeling of delight
Shall rear her form to stately height
Her virgin bosom swell;
Such thoughts to Lucy I will give
While she and I together live
Here in this happy dell

Dorothy's journals were to restore to memory scenes that he recreated in poems such as "I Wandered Lonely as a Cloud". Her sensitive response encouraged him to write on natural subjects, which were condemned as trivial by fashionable reviewers. To quote:

Wordsworth was in all things fortunate, but in nothing more fortunate than in this, that so unique a companion should have been ready to devote herself to Him with an affection wholly free from egotism or jealousy—an affection that yearned only to satisfy his subtlest needs, and to transfuse all that was best in herself into larger being.[2]

Thus, Dorothy was a direct link with his childhood. Her presence carried him back to the mystical exaltations of the childhood days.

Coleridge

Besides his sister Dorothy the only other person that Wordsworth acknowledged as having a hand in his recovery and as influencing his intellect, was Coleridge. Wordsworth was highly indebted to Coleridge and his sister. Wordsworth acknowledged with gratitude the debt he owed to Colèridge by dedicating to him his autobiographical poem, *The Prelude*:

O capacious Soul
Placed on this earth to live and understand,
And from thy presence shed the light of love,

Shall I be mute, ere thou be spoken of?
The kindred influence to my heart of hearts
Did also find its way.

(*The Prelude* XIV, 277-82)

Wordsworth's friendship with Coleridge quickened his critical power and taught him to study the working of his own imagination in a more conscious and detached manner. Coleridge was one of those men in whose presence it is difficult to be ordinary. "In their endless talk the expansive mind of Coleridge must have invigorated his comrade's entire intellectual being. The friendship rapidly matured into close intimacy, and the genius of both poets burst into full bloom."[3] He had that generosity of temper, which rouses others to their proper greatness. The mere sound of his voice was the "music of thought".

Coleridge had placed Wordsworth's feet into the path of philosophy. In 1807 Wordsworth would have seemed to be advancing in a sure and straight course. The withdrawal of Coleridge's influence carried with the music of thought for Wordsworth kind of relapse into ordinariness. This feeling is described in the following poem:

There is a change—and I am poor;
Your love hath been, nor long ago,
A fountain at my fond heart's door,
Whose only business was to flow;
And flow it did; not taking heed
Of its own bounty, or my need.
What happy moments did I count!
Blest was I then all bliss above!

Social Influences

The influence of a number of persons, including some of his friends and contemporary events on him cannot be ruled out. At school, he mingled with his school equals, sons of yeomen, or of professional men, a feeling of equality still existed in the Dales of his boyhood. Wordsworth's friends were poor simple schoolboys but he found them "hung round with honours and importance". Wordsworth was happy to exchange memories with Edward Birkett and Fietcher Raincock.

In his own college, he found another familiar freshman, Thomas Law Throb who had come from Sedbeigh for a final year at Hawkshead before going up to the university. He had lived with Wordsworth at Ann Iyson's cottage. Wordsworth was better prepared academically than most freshmen. In his time Hawkshead gained many triumph in the university Exam at the Senate House.

At Cambridge, the desolate and lonely part of his college life marked by frequent flights to the fields, was soon replaced by companionships and friendship.

We sauntered, played, or rioted;
We talked unprofitable talk at morning hours.

(*The Prelude* III, 248-49)

At first, Wordsworth had first become conscious of his love for Hawkshead, the place and its people whose occupation really he loved. His new sense of mission clarified his relationship to the university:

I was detached
Internally from academic cares
From every hope of powers & reward

And wished to be a lodger in that house
Of letters and no more.

The death of his brother John in 1805 changed the whole current of his thought. The death of his son Thomas made him ten years older than his age. Only the death of his little Catharine inspired the most poignant sonnet in English literature. Among other persons, the influence of Coleridge and Dorothy gave a new direction to Wordsworth's life.

Literary Influences

Wordsworth was a voracious reader. Books were the best source of his intellectual strength. His wide reading brought him in intimacy with a number of philosophers and thinkers who influenced his outlook in one way or the other. The poets who influenced him most in later years were Cambridge men, and in *The Prelude,* Book III, he recalls some of their names. So of Spenser he writes:

Sweet Spenser. Moving through his clouded heaven
With the moon's beauty and the moon's soft pace.

(*The Prelude* III, 280-81)

Wordsworth was highly influenced by Milton. In fact, Milton was his great idol. We may not find Miltonic loftiness but Miltonic purity is found in *The Prelude* and several other poems of Wordsworth. While describing the purpose of *The Prelude,* he says:

May my life
Express the image of a better time,
More wise desires and simpler manners.

These lines carry an echo of saints who carry within them an inalienable assurance of their own poetic salvation. Thus they are the deliberate reminiscences of Milton. *The Prelude* is built in and round that grand conception of the nature of the poetic art to which Milton has given in "The Reason of Church Government", immortal expression. The portrait of Milton is intimate and personal:

I seemed to see him here
Familiarly, and in his scholar's dress
Bounding before me-yet a stripling youth
A boy, no better, with his rosy cheeks
Angelical, keen eye, courageous look,
And conscious step of purity and pride.

(*The Prelude* III, 287-92)

He recalls too that Chaucer's Tales were set:

Beside the pleasant Mill of Tropmpington
I laughed with Chaucer; in the hawthorn shade
Heard him, while birds were warbling, tell his tales
of amorous passion.

(*The Prelude* III, 275-78)

The influence of some eminent thinkers is also evident in Wordsworth's works:

Rousseau

In the opinion of Legouis, Wordsworth is intellectually "a son of Rousseau". Likewise, Harper also contends that Rousseau's works have traces of influence on Wordsworth's poetry. There is little doubt that Wordsworth must have read Rousseau's *Confessions* and *Emile.* Consequently, in his "Descriptive Sketches" and the "Letter to the Bishop of Liandaff", Wordsworth uses the language of Rousseau. It is difficult to determine the extent to which Rousseau may have influenced Wordsworth. Far more than any other man of letters, either of antiquity, modern times Wordsworth has been highly influenced by this great man Rousseau.

Wordsworth uses the language of Rousseau to express his radical sentiments. It shows that Wordsworth was familiar with Rousseau. In "The Convention of Cintra" and "The Borderers", he mentions the philosopher by name. The influence of Rousseau is also seen in Wordsworth's preference for the rustic as against the urban. The introspective pre-occupation with time and memory in Rousseau's *Confessions* and *Reveries of a Solitary Walker* foreshadows Wordsworth's time consciousness in *The Prelude.*

Newton

Wordsworth had deep veneration for Newton whose discoveries Wordsworth looked upon as "the Grandest ever known". This is Newton's conception of subtle spirits and active principles in Nature which seems to be echoed in a passage of one of his book, *The Excursion,* in which he affirms that "To every form of being is assigned... An active Principle". In the same passage "the Soul of all the worlds" reminds one of Newton's "Being incorporeal...in infinite Space". The following lines of "Tintern Abbey" also remind the principle of Newton:

A motion and spirit, that impels
All thinking things, all objects of all thoughts,
And rolls through all things.

In The Prelude, he describes Newton's statue:

Of Newton with his prism and silent face,
The marble index of a mind for ever
Voyaging through strange seas of Thought, alone.

(*The Prelude* III, 61-63)

Locke

Wordsworth had a favourable opinion of Locke's works. It would have been wise for Wordsworth to read Locke's *Essay* in the spring of 1789, for a good knowledge of it was considered essential for an English gentleman. He once remarked that the influence of Locke's *Essay* was not due to its merits, which are considerable; but to external circumstances. It came forth at a happy opportunity, and coincided with the prevalent opinion of the time.

The influence of other ideas of Locke, as distinguished from those of Hartley, is difficult to trace. Perhaps Locke's historical plain method contributed to the realistic strain in Wordsworth's poetry. The interest of mental tablet moved Wordsworth to read Locke's *Essay*, when it was assigned to him. Certainly at Cambridge where Locke was the starting point of so much that it was thought and said:

> *"Wordsworth could not have escaped its influence. Locke's doctrine which derived all our knowledge from sensation was capable of serving Wordsworth, who imbibed it through Hartley as a philosophic sanction for his own deep rooted instincts and furnished him with it at least a foundation for his conscious poetic theory."*[4]

Hartley

The association of Hartley had a considerable impact on Wordsworth's poetic genius. *The Prelude* and "The Tintern Abbey" echo with the conceptions and phraseology of Hartley. In *The Prelude* I, we have a distinct statement of how the principle of association worked to build up the mental life of the poet out of the materials provided by the senses. Wordsworth refers to this theory when he mentions in his Preface that his purpose is "above all" to make "the incidents and situations of common life" interesting by tracing in them, truly though not ostentatiously, the primary laws of our nature; chiefly, as far as regards the manners in which we associate ideas in a state of excitement. To quote:

> *"What attracted Wordsworth to Hartley was, for one thing, the insistence on physical sensations as the starting point of the process of intellectual and moral development. This appealed to Wordsworth's realism, his disposition to refer to the world of senses as the standard of reality, to work from the natural towards the spiritual. "*[5]

Kant

Wordsworth must have come under the influence of Kant through Coleridge. He came to have an acquaintance with the doctrines of Kant during his conversations with Coleridge. The following lines of Wordsworth's "Ode to Duty" echo with the Kantian philosophy:

Stern Lawgiver! yet thou dost wear
The God head's most benignant grace;
Nor know we anything so fair
As is the smile upon thy face:
Flowers laugh before thee on their beds
And fragrance in thy footing treads;
Thou dost preserve the stars from wrong;
And the most ancient heavens, through Thee, are fresh and strong.

(Ode to Duty, 41-48)

The German philosopher similarly compared the austere sublimity of the stars with the categorical imperative and maintained that moral law is binding upon all thinking beings including God.

Likewise, following Kant's concept of a Kingdom of Ends, Wordsworth summarized the doctrine that every rational creature should be treated as an end in the *Excursion*. To quote him:

Our life is turned
Out of her course, wherever man is made
An offering, or a sacrifice, a tool
Or implement, a passive thing employed
As a brute mean, without acknowledgement
Of common right or interest in the end;
Used or abused, as selfishness may prompt.

Thus the poet appears to have accepted two main principles of Kantian ethics; the categorical imperative and the doctrine of ends.

Spinoza

During the days of his closest intimacy with Wordsworth, Coleridge must often have discovered about the philosophy of Spinoza. Wordsworth found in Spinoza's theory intermediate between Godwin's mechanistic determinism and Coleridge's doctrine of free will. As a bridge, Spinoza's philosophy enabled him to cling to his intense naturalism and social idealism while he moved towards his later libertarian convictions. Although the poetry of Wordsworth's later years shows his divergence from Spinoza, it bears some traces of his earlier creed.

Berkeley

Among the later English Empiricists, Berkeley maintained that the vivid qualitative features of the natural world are generally real. Wordsworth was impressed by one of his doctrines that we see God in the same way that we see a man. In Berkeley's *Alciphron,* the sense of sacredness, which had traditionally been associated with the supernatural, became attached to nature itself. The essence of the Wordsworthian revolution is precisely this transfer of the "numinous" from the remote heavenly sphere to:

> *...the very world, which is the world.*
> *Of all of us the place where in the end,*
> *We find our happiness or not at all.*

(French Revolution, 38-40)

This revolution can be illustrated by typical passages from Wordsworth's poetry:

> *Listen! The mighty Being is awake,*
> *And doth with his eternal motion make*
> *A sound like thunder-everlastingly.*

(It is a Beauteous Evening Calm and Free, 6-8)

To express the influence of Berkeley on Wordsworth, Melvin Rader writes:

> *"In combining, a sensationist theory of knowledge with an immanent theism Berkley may have contributed substantially to Wordsworth's religion of nature. Whether the poet ever carefully studied Berkley's works at first hand is immaterial, since, Coleridge must have conveyed their import to him in conversations."*[6]

Platonism

Coleridge communicated to Wordsworth many Platonic conceptions. He refers to Plato's "genius", his "lore sublime", and the "everlasting praise" that is his due. A careful examination of Wordsworth's poetry shows that some of his doctrines bear the Platonic stamp. According to Plato's scheme, the universe is not only a rational universe, but God himself is eternal Reason. The following lines, from *The Prelude* show this Platonic scheme:

Wisdom and Spirit of the universe;
Thou Soul that art the eternity of thought.
That giv'st to forms and images a breath
And everlasting motion.

(*The Prelude I*, 401-04)

Plato maintained that reason is one with spiritual love. Likewise, Wordsworth maintains that imagination and intellectual love are identical with "reason in her most exalted mood". In the same way, Wordsworth also believed in Plato's concept of a Soul of the World. About the influence of Plato on Wordsworth, Melvin Rader observes:

"Wordsworth is in vital accord with Plato in his 'Intimation of Immortality'. Not only did he make use, in the famous Ode, of the Platonic 'recollection' of pre-existence, but the entire poem follows the Pheado in emphasizing the 'high instincts' by which our 'mortal Nature' appears a pensioner upon the immortal elements of mind.[7]

To conclude, Wordsworth was a bold and romantic thinker. He granted ideas from many sources and adapted them freely to his own purposes. Many political thinkers and philosophers exerted their influences on Wordsworth's ideas, but he was far too great to be enslaved to any political or philosophical movement. His own experience of life was by far the most important source of his ideas; next to this was the living presence of Dorothy and Coleridge; finally, there was the influence of books, and among these he roamed far and wide.

References

1. Edited by C.H.H., *The Ages of Wordsworth,* Preface to second Edition, October, 1897, p. 166.

2. Myers, F.W.H., *Wordsworth,* Macmillan & Co. Ltd., London, 1912, pp. 27-28.

3. Melvin Rader, *Wordsworth- A Philosophical Approach,* O.U.P., London, 1967, p. 9.

4. Willey, Basil, *The Seventeenth Century Background,* Chatto & Windus, London, 1949, p. 294.

5. Beach, Joseph Warren, *The Concept of Nature in Nineteenth Century English Poetry,* Russell & Russell, New York, 1966, p. 130.

6. Rader, Melvin, "*Wordsworth—A Philosophical Approach*", p. 47.

7. *Ibid.,* p. 79.

4

Wordsworth's Views on Poetry

Different critics, from ancient eminent Aristotle, Horace, Longinus, Dante, etc., to Sidney, Tasso, Dryden, Johnson, Wordsworth, Coleridge, Arnold, etc., to modern critics, all have defined poetry in their own way. They suggest the end of poetry, this or that, but obviously joy, teaching, power to move, etc., are considered the main objects of poetry. The word poetry is still occasionally used as a synonym of verse. "But of course, many who do not consider that all poetry must be written in verse, i.e., regard verse as an indispensable accident, though not the differentia."[1] One common element implied or explicit is "Poetry speech is somehow extraordinary. The problem of defining poetry is the problem of defining its extraordinariness."[2] Among all authorities defining poetry, Wordsworth's conception is much more acceptable and heart-touching. This chapter presents an analysis of Wordsworth's conception of poetry.

Wordsworth was the first to maintain that "all good poetry is the spontaneous overflow of power feelings".[3] It means poetry cannot be composed under duress nor can the poet be forced to write at the spur of an opportune moment. Poetry is a matter of feeling and mood. When the poetic mood is on, the poet sings out songs of rapture or sorrow spontaneously from the core of his heart. In a poetic mood, poetry flows out naturally from the poet's heart. His language of discourse in such moments becomes the language of poetic inspiration. Thus, according to Wordsworth, deep emotion is the fundamental aspect of poetry. Without emotion and powerful feelings, poetry cannot be written. Sensibility alone is, however, not sufficient to ensure good poetry; it must be directed and modified by a calm mind.

Wordsworth's aim was thus morally serious and intellectually controlled. If we say that his definition of poetry as "the spontaneous overflow of powerful feelings" was a call to uncontrolled emotion, it is to misinterpret his purpose. In eighteenth century sense "Spontaneous" means to achieve something by an act of free will. The poet's greater responsiveness to experience and his capacity to think "long and deeply" distinguishes him from mere versifier. This emphasis on the recreation of experience gave rise to Wordsworth's statement that in his poetry the feeling therein developed gives importance to action and situation and not the action and situation to the feeling. Thus says Wordsworth: "Poetry is produced by a man, who being possessed of more than organic sensibility, has also thought long and deeply." From this statement rises the second contention of Wordsworth, that is, "Poetry takes its origin from emotion recollected in tranquility."[4]

Wordsworth explains the role of calm thinking and deliberate contemplation in the composition of poetry. Later on, in the Preface, he says,

"The emotion is contemplated till by a species of reaction, the

tranquility gradually disappears and an emotion kindred to that which was before the subject of contemplation, is gradually produced; and does itself actually exist in the mind. In this mood successful composition generally begins and in a mood similar to this it is carried on."[5]

The process of poetic composition is not an easy one. As expressed in the above statement, poetic composition has to pass through four stages: recollection, contemplation, recrudescence and composition. To quote Herbert Read:

"That good poetry is never an immediate reaction to the provoking cause; that our sensations must be allowed time to sink back into the common fund of our experience, there to find their level and due proportion. That level is found for them by and then in the union of contemplating mind and the receiving sensibility raises that unique mood of expression which we call poetry."[6]

In his Preface to the *Poems of 1815,* Wordsworth himself has indicated the process which is involved in poetic creation:

"The power requisite for the production of poetry are: First, those of Observation and Description, i.e., the ability to observe with accuracy things as they are in themselves and with fidelity to describe them, unmodified by any passion or feeling existing in the mind of describer; whether the things depicted be actually present to the senses or have a place only in the memory. . . . Secondly, Sensibility, which the more requisite it is, the wider will be the range of a poet's perceptions and the more will he be incited to observe objects both as they exist in themselves and as reacted upon by his own mind. Thirdly, Reflection, which makes the poet acquainted with the value of actions, images, thoughts and feelings and assists the sensibility in perceiving their connection with each other. Fourthly, Imagination and Fancy, to modify, to create and

to associate. Fifthly, Invention, by which characters are composed out of materials supplied by observation whether of the poet's own heart and mind or of external life and nature. And lastly Judgement—to decide how and where and in what degree, each of these faculties ought to be exerted. . . . By judgement, also, is determined what are the laws and appropriate graces of every species of composition."[7]

Wordsworth actually followed the above process of poetic composition. He allowed the emotions to sink and revived them at a later stage in a state of tranquility. "*The Prelude*", "Daffodils", "Tintern Abbey", "Resolution and Independence", "The Solitary Reaper", etc., were composed according to emotion recollected in tranquility. "He indulged his memory with long periods of reverie, set it to travel to and fro among the past experiences of his life and loved solitude and indolence chiefly because during the lulls of social intercourse and intellectual labour lost impressions were recaptured". He loved to set in "the long barren silence" contemplating the submerged feelings and images in his mind, taking hold of them, when they rose to the surface. His own function, as it seemed to him was simply that of a still and patient chronicler. He speaks of himself as being "not used to make a present joy the matter of a song". He tells us in the Epilogue to the Waggoner that it was his habit to keep a theme in his mind for years before putting it into verse. He speaks of

Nor it is I who play the part,
But a shy spirit in my heart
That comes and goes, will sometimes leap
From hiding places ten years deep:
Of haunts me familiar face
Returning, like a host unlaid;
Until the debt I owe be paid.

Here we encounter a doctrine, which is part and parcel of Wordsworth's theory of poetic inspiration. Wordsworth could follow his theory of poetic composition, but to say that all poetry is written in a state of calm and tranquil recollections is not true. If that is accepted, the scope of lyric poetry will be limited. The poetry will not be written at the white heat of emotional excitement. Hence to compose poetry in the style referred to by Wordsworth one needs a fine memory that can faithfully recollect the past and a contemplative mind fit to cogitate and recreate what had been experienced at an early stage. Wordsworth could succeed in his aim for he had been endowed by nature with a prodigious memory and a contemplative mind. For other poets like Shelley, the method of Wordsworth could not be applied. It was applicable to him alone. He alone had the gift of visualizing the past with a wonderful vividness and float over them with the fancy of a poet:

For oft when on my couch I lie
In vacant or in pensive mood.
They flash upon that inward eye
Which is the bliss of solitude.

(Daffodiles)

Wordsworth believes with Aristotle that "poetry is the most philosophic of all writing . . . its object is truth not individual and local, but general and operative". It is universal truth carried alive into the heart by passion. Passion or emotion is the central principle in and through which the poet seeks to understand, interpret and express his experience, observations and meditations of human life. Passion has a tendency to unify, to bring the entire universe into a grand unity. Consequently there is the representation of life in all poetry. If thus argued, "Poetry is the image of man and nature."[8]

Poetry is not a mere discussion, nor a dish for epicurean taste. It is according to Wordsworth, "the breath and finer spirit of all knowledge, the impassioned expression which is in the countenance of all science. Poetry seeks to ennoble and edify. It is like the morning star which throws its radiance through the gloom and darkness of life. Poetry has its value

"In framing models to improve the scheme of man's existence and recast the world."

(*The Excursion* III, 336-37)

Poetry is the instrument of the propagation of moral thoughts. Wordsworth's poetry does not simply delight us but it also teaches us deep moral lessons and brings home to us deep philosophic truths about life and religion. A poetry of revolt against life; a poetry of indifference towards moral ideas is a poetry of indifference towards life. "Poetry is the first and last of all knowledge. It is as immortal as the heart of man."

Wordsworth condemned the commonly accepted theory of poetry calling it false and vicious as it was artificial and stilted. Its spirit was also wholly wrong and mistaken as it had no hold on nature and common life. Wordsworth was of the view that common life also has the sufficient interest to inspire the noblest achievements of a poet, and that Nature must be observed with unflinching fidelity if she was to be described with truth or freshness. He asks why poetry should be

A history only of departed things,
Or a mere fiction of what never was?
For the discerning intellect of Man,
When wedded to this goodly universe
In love and holy passion, shall find these
A simple produce of the common day.

I, long before the blissful hour arrives,
Would chant, in lonely peace, the spousal hour
Of this great consummation: and by words
Which speak of nothing more than what we are
Would I arouse the sensual from their sleep
Of Death, and win the vacant and the vain
To noble raptures; while my voice proclaims
How exquisitely the individual mind
(And the progressive powers perhaps no less
Of the whole species) to the external world
Is fitted: and how exquisitely too-
Theme this but little heard of among men-
The external world is fitted to the mind.

(Recluse)

This noble passage presents Wordsworth's peculiar view of poetry. He announces a return to simplicity, to simple themes and simple language and teaches that a true poet finds sufficient inspiration in the simplest sights of life and Nature. He speaks only what we are, and is prepared to write nothing that is not justified by the actual truth of things. He sets himself against that species of poetry that finds its impulse and passion in morbid or exaggerated sentiment. To him the "meanest flower that blows can give thoughts that do often lie too deep for tears", and by preserving his soul in poetry which will affect even the lowliest of men, because it is expressed in the plain and unadorned language of common life.

Whether Wordsworth followed his theory of poetry or not, is another question. It is said that occasionally his theory of poetry itself breaks down. Even in 1798, he departs from his theories in order to obtain his most striking poetical successes. The unusual range of his creative sensibility is visible in *Lyrical Ballads*. The poems such as "Expostulation and Reply", "the Tables Turned", "To My Sister", "Ode to Duty" and even "Tintern Abbey" belie his theory of poetry.

References

1. *Dictionary of World Literary Terms* (ed.), Joseph T. Shipley, p. 243.
2. *Ibid.*, p. 242.
3. "Preface to the *Lyrical Ballads*", *Wordsworth: Poetical Works* (ed.), E.D. Selincourt, p. 740.
4. *Ibid.*
5. *Ibid.*, p. 740.
6. Read, Herbert, *Wordsworth*, London, Faber and Faber Limited, pp. 112-13.
7. Preface to the Edition of 1815, *Wordsworth: Poetical Works* (ed.), E.D. Selincourt, p. 752.
8. Preface to the *Lyrical Ballads*, 1802, quoted in *Selections from Wordsworth* (ed.), Ifor Evans, p. 192.

5

Wordsworth's Views on Poet

While discussing the concept of poetry it is a must to analyze the concept of poet also, as poetry exists only because of a poet. As of poetry, various critics have expressed their views on poet also. Here we are concerned with Wordsworth's views, so a brief conception of Wordsworth's views on poet has been presented in this chapter. In his "Preface" (1802), Wordsworth asks, "What is a Poet"? He himself replies:

> *"He is a man speaking to men: a man it is true, endowed with more lively sensibility, more enthusiasm and tenderness, who has a greater knowledge of human nature, and a more comprehensive soul than are supposed to be common among mankind; a man pleased with his own passions and volitions and who rejoices more than other men in the spirit of life that is in him delighting to contemplate similar volitions and passions as manifested in goings-on of the universe and habitually impelled to create them where he does not find them. To these qualities he has added a disposition to be affected more than other men by absent things as if they were present; an ability of conjuring up in himself passions, which*

are indeed far from being the same as those produced by real events."[1]

Wordsworth's views about a poet present several aspects of the personality of a poet. He is not a great singer only, he is not a man living in an ivory tower and lost in the subtleties of his own emotions, beyond the comprehension of common people. It does not mean that he is an ordinary man. But he is one man among men who speaks quietly what most moves his heart and what is most central to his deeper thoughts on the interrelations of man, nature and transcendental. Anyone cannot sit down and write great poetry if he happens to feel something. In fact, the poet has a distinctive imaginative faculty which enables him to conjure up passions different from ordinary beings. He has more tenderness, enthusiasm and knowledge than the common man. He is more articulate and has a deeper capacity for delight in all he sees and knows. He differs from common men not in kind, but in degree. He may not be a favourite for divine afflatus, set apart from his kind in lordly magnificence. He is not a frenzied enthusiast or hierophant writing better than he knows. It is this extra gift of imaginative sympathy and sensitive intelligence that makes him able to write about things which other men only dimly feel.

"The Poet", says Wordsworth, "writes under one restriction only, namely, the necessity of giving immediate pleasure to human being possessed of that information which may be expected from him, not as a lawyer, a physician, a mariner, an astronomer or a natural philosopher, but as a Man."[2] The poet must take care that whatever passion he communicates to his reader, those passions, if his readers mind be sound and vigorous, should always be accompanied by an overbalance of pleasure. Now it becomes clear that the poet should communicate to his reader, not that passion in which he himself began but that filtered passion that is full of pleasure. Thus Wordsworth rehabilitates pleasure to a primary position. The neo-classical school—Horace, Scaliger, and Boileau—held that the immediate pleasure the poet communicates is directly derived sincere apprehension of the "beauty of the universe" arising from his habit to look at the world "in a spirit of love". Far from being a degradation of the poet's art, the necessity of producing immediate pleasure "is a homage paid to the native and naked dignity of man to the grand elementary principle of pleasure, by which he knows and feels and lives and moves".

A poet is no longer a "social" instrument but an individual pleased with his own passions and volitions. He is not a mere copier but a creator. He is a man with Sn intense sensibility, not rationality. He is no longer interested in manners or in city life. He wants poetry to deal with the "essential passions of the heart" and for that man in nature is a better subject than man in the city. Here, Wordsworth emphasis on three attributes of a poet, not on the apex but in the lower ranges where he differs from other men. The three attribute which Wordsworth enumerates are—intense sensibility, comprehensive soul and his power to create.

A poet, according to Wordsworth, has a noble mission to carry out. In spite of his distinct individuality, he has to perform a definite social and moral role. A great poet is out to rectify men's feelings, to give them new compositions of feeling, to render their feelings more sane, pure and permanent, in short, more consonant to nature; that is to eternal nature and the great moving spirit of things. His work is intended to humble and humanize the readers in order that they may be purified and exalted.

The poet is a teacher and through the medium of poetry he imparts moral lesson for the betterment of human life. In other words, the poet should teach the great lesson of how to live in society and he should at the same time offer both an emotional and rational gratification to the human mind.With regard to the ideal poet, Wordsworth remarks that "the poet is chiefly distinguished from other men by a great promptness to think and feel without immediate external excitement and a greater power in expressing such thoughts and feelings as are produced in him in hat manner...the poet thinks and feels in the spirit of human passions... poets do not write for poets alone but for men... the poet must descend from this supposed height; and in order to excite rational sympathy, he must express himself as other men express themselves."[3]

The poet feels in a fashion livelier, more poignant than ordinary man. Because he is a poet, he more quickly than ordinary men reestablishes his tranquility. He "passions" again. The sorrow that has slept, stirs anew; but now it is

> *Sorrow that is not sorrow but delight And miserable love that is not pain To hear of.*

Poetry gains the power of consolation only because of this purified passion that the poet conveys to those to whom he speaks. Wordsworth has a peculiar way of expressing his feelings. The purpose of poetic creation is vain unless the passion of thought and feeling has the power of spiritualizing. When he writes, "Poets do not write for Poets alone but for men",[4] he means to say that they do not live by taking in one another's tricks, quaintness, hieroglyphics and enigmas but by the bread of a common humanity.

"The poet must descend from his supposed height." remarks Garrod, "that the office of the poet is prophecy that he belongs to an order of men who are rapt, possessed, uttering more than they know".[5] Wordsworth was as well aware as other poets who have brought into greater display that element of poetry, which consists in ecstasy. The poet must have certain gifts that are not common among mankind. Thus Wordsworth emphasizes on the individualism of the poet. The poet has that pleasure in "his own passions and volitions" which makes him different from the social poet of other periods.

It is said that the dimension of a poet's imagination is beyond thinking. A poet can reach where even the sun cannot reach. Wordsworth also holds the same opinion about a poet. To quote Wordsworth:

> *"The poet is the rock of defence for human nature; an upholder and preserver, carrying everywhere with him relationship and love. In spite of difference of soil and climate, of language and manners, of laws and customs, in spite of things silently gone out of mind and things violently destroyed, the Poet binds together by passion and knowledge; of the vast empire of human society, as it is spread over the whole earth and over all time."*[6]

The poet is to keep his eye on the object for the purpose of revealing, not the exterior of the object, but its essence. The poet then must keep more than his eye on the external object. Wordsworth's comment on the poet that "the poet has a greater knowledge of human nature and a more comprehensive soul", echoes Dryden's appreciation of Shakespeare and this same was the criteria of Johnson's verdict on Shakespeare.

Wordsworth has given a detailed description of qualities required for a poet. He regards observation, description, sensibility, reflection, imagination, invention and judgement as qualities requisite to a poet. He has also clarified these qualities such, "Sensibility, which the more exquisite, it is the wider will be the range of a poet's perceptions; and the more will he be incited to observe objects, both as they exist in themselves and as re-acted by his own mind." The poet brings to the work of observation a more lively sensibility than other men.

Not only in "Prefaces" but in poetry also Wordsworth has described the growth of a poet's mind. In *The Prelude* his sentiments are equal to Eric Gill—The artist is not a special sort of man but every man is a special sort of artist. When he recalls his early formative experiences, he reacts with special sensitiveness to the great moments of exaltation in any ordinary childhood. In the *Lyrical Ballads*, the subjects of his poems were taken from ordinary life. "They were designed to raise that quickened response to daily existence which it was thought had been besmirched by 'the lethargy of custom'."

Wordsworth's poems inspired their audience to see the world freshly, sympathetically and naturally like his old Cumberland beggar who stirred the charitable impulses of those around him. He awakened in public that sense of community which is the special power of the poet speaking as a man to man. It was really a daring attempt to express the universal experience of ordinary people at a time of political reaction.

Comparison of Wordsworth's poet with other notable representatives of mankind shows that the poet is "the embodiment of an Idea, secondly as agent in an action, thirdly as a man speaking to men and lastly in his human relationship, that society of men to whom and for whom he will speak".[7] In the first 271 lines of *The Prelude,* the poet is revealed as made in the image of his Maker. The poet of Wordsworth is verily another Adam, man from the clay. He is tempted by circumstances to renounce the life of obedient joy for a curious search into the knowledge of good and evil. His distinctly human trait is that he has the power to create from the first breath of the "vital soul" to the last.

Even as an agent of the one great mind,
Creates, creator and receiver both.
... Such, verily, is the first
poetic spirit of our human life.

Wordsworth also presents his poet like the traditional Christ, invested with the burden and glory of teaching. A kind of restorative psychology and pedagogy can be seen in *The Prelude*. Wordsworth is of the view that admiration of a true poet is admiration of mankind; for the poet possesses in unusual concentration the powers present in ordinary man. "A Poet is not set apart by unique or peculiar talents; to the contrary, the highest reach of genius is to recognize and reflect the kinship of the artist (poet) with men of other walks."[8]

Thus, Wordsworth provides a high place to the poet. In fact, a great poet is not an ordinary occurrence. The advent of great poetry is not like the delivery of milk and bread, so a great poet is a challenge.

References

1. Preface to the *Lyrical Ballads*, 1802, quoted in *Selections from Wordsworth* (ed.), Ifor Evans, p. 190.
2. Preface, *Selection from Wordsworth* (ed.), Ifor Evans, p. 192.
3. *Ibid.*, pp. 195-96.
4. *Ibid.*, p. 196.
5. Garrod, H.W., *Wordsworth,* Lectures and Essays, p. 168.
6. Preface, *Selection from Wordsworth* (ed.), Ifor Evans, p. 194.
7. Potts, Abbie Findlay, *Wordsworth's Prelude: A Study of Its Literary Form,* New York, Ithaca, Cornwell University Press, p. 339.
8. Carl, Woodring, Wordsworth, Cambridge, Harvard University Press, p. 145.

6

Lake District

Lake District is the soul of Wordsworth's poetry. Wordsworth's love of nature is the precious gift of the region where he was born and brought up. The rich description of natural beauty scattered through the poetry of Wordsworth gives a detailed description of Lake District. He had so much love for this region that he was not satisfied by just a poetic description of this region so he wrote *A Guide through the District of the Lakes*. Here he describes each and every mountain, valley, lakes and other aspects and also a detailed description of the way to reach it.

Topographical View

This sublime and beautiful region with all its hidden treasures provides immense pleasure. Situated in the North of England, Lake District is enclosed and surrounded by lakes, vales and mountains. Somewhat stretched between two mountains Great Gavel and Scawfell, there are a number of valleys not fewer than eight rivers, streams and lakes. These valleys are spread in a circle like the spokes from the nave of a wheel. Among these places there are dwelling places, all around with lakes and streams. A short description of these is given below.

First, there is the Vale of Langdale which has the long lake of Winandermere stretched nearly to the sea. From the south-east towards the south, the Vale of Coniston can be seen. This valley does not form the nave of the wheel. When we go towards the west, we see immediately at our feet the Vale of Duddon. It has a copious stream winding among fields, rocks and mountains and terminating its course in the sands of Duddon. The fourth vale is the Vale of Esk. Though it has the same characteristics as the last, yet beautifully discriminated from it by its peculiar features its stream passes under the woody steep upon which stands Muncaster Castle. Its stream, after forming a short and foaming aestuary, enters the sea below the small town of Ravenglass. Next Vale is the deep valley of Wastdale. It is in mathematical figure with its little chapel and half a dozen neat dwellings scattered upon a plain of meadow. The long, narrow, stern and desolate lake of Wastdale lies beyond this little fertile plain, within a bed of Steep Mountain. A stream named Irt also issues from Wast water and falls into the aestuary of the river Esk. Then comes the Vale of Ennerdale, with its lake of somewhat bold and savage shores. It has a stream named Ehen or Enna. Flowing through a soft and fertile country, it assumes the form of a river. It breaks through the barrier of sand and enters the Irish Sea. Next comes the Vale of Buttermere, with the lake and village of that name. The Vale of Lorton has the stream named Coker which is lost in the Derwent, below the noble ruins of Cockermouth Castle. Lastly, there is the Vale of Borrowdale, of which the vale of Keswick, is only a continuation. It stretches due north and brings us to a point nearly opposite to the vale of Winandermere with which we began. Thus it presents the image of a wheel, thus far exact, is little more than one half complete. The deficiency of this wheel on the eastern side is completed by the Vales of Wytheburn, Ulswater, Hawswater and the Vale of Grasmere and Rydal but none of these vales falls between Great Gavel and Scawfell. These vales have their own streams and lakes. This is the general topographical view of the country of the lakes in the north of England. Several ridges enclose these vales and divide them from each other, that is, in the forms and surfaces, "first of the swelling grounds, next of the hills and rocks, and lastly of the mountains—an ascent of almost regular gradation, from elegance and richness, to their highest point of grandeur and sublimity."[1] These hills and valleys have every possible embellishment of beauty, dignity and splendour which light and shadow can bestow upon these diversified objects. Besides this, though from a point, between Great Gavel and Scawfell, a shepherd can descent into any one of eight of the principal vales, not more than an hour; but the scene changes from north to south. For example, in the vale of Winandermere, which is southward, if the spectator looks for gentle and lovely scenes; towards the north that is in the Vale of Keswick the scene is directly the reverse. When a spectator standing on the shores or the breast of Winandermere sees the setting of the sun, he finds that some of the summits of the loftiest mountains "half or wholly hidden by clouds or by the blaze of light which the orb diffuses around it and the surface of the lake will reflect before the eye correspondent colours through every variety of beauty and through all degrees of splendour".[2] At the same time, in the Vale of Keswick, the sun sets over the humbler regions of the landscape and showers down upon them the radiance which at once veils and glorifies. Broad streams of rosy crimson, purple or golden light illuminate the grand mountains in the south and south-east. Besides it, an intermixture of solemn shadows is seen distinctly through a cool and clear atmosphere.

In order to know the beauty of Lake District, we should know its features step by step. Let us first see the beauty of mountains. Their forms are endlessly diversified. They may be inferior in individual magnitude and grandeur, but in the combination which they make towering above each other, or lifting themselves in ridges like the waves of a tumultuous sea and in the beauty and variety of their surfaces and colours, they are surpassed by none. As regards to the general surface of the mountains, it is rich and green by the moisture of the climate in some places, rocks predominate. In the ridge that divides Eskdale freom Wasdale, granite is found. Generally the colours of this rocky part are bluish or hoary grey. It is called schist by mineralogists. There are various types of herbage and plants on these mountains to decorate them. These "mountains are of height sufficient to have the surface towards the summit softened by distance and to imbibe the finest aerial hues".[3] Many rich colours play into each other over the surface of the mountains.

Though the valleys have been represented under the general image of the spokes of a wheel, they are, for the most part winding and these winding are abrupt and intricate. These valleys are sometimes divided from each other by a mutual approximation of the hills. The bottom of these valleys is mostly a spacious and gently declining area. Sometimes it is level as the floor of a temple or sometimes it is the surface of a lake and broken in many cases by rocks and hills, which rise up like islands from the plain. The beauty of the rocks and hills scattered over the plain of the vale is often much heightened by a single cottage or cluster of cottages.

When we come to the lakes of the region, we find a kind of perfection in them. The most favourable characteristics of the lakes of this country is that when the whole length of these lakes is seen from an elevated point, they lose some what of the peculiar form of the lake and assume the resemblance of magnificent river such as Windermere, Ulswater, Hawkswater. In spite of their winding form, one lake may in succession present to the eye the essential characteristics of many. Sometimes the same vale furnishes a succession of lakes instead of being filled with one. "As the comparatively small size of the lakes in the North of England is favourable to the production of variegated landscape, their boundary line also is for the most part gracefully or boldly indented."[4] Masses of rocks that have been precipitated from the heights into the area of waters lie in some places like stranded ships. Between the margin of the lake and the mountains, there is sometimes gently sloping lawns and woods or sometimes flat and fertile meadows. In the midst of this beautiful surrounding, one may see several birds that enliven the waters. Wild-ducks in springtime hatch their young in the islands; the sandpiper attracts the eye by its restless motion, flitting along the stony margins. The stately heron seems to have caught delicate hue from the blue waters. In winter, lakes are full of wild swans, widgeons, Goldings and other aquatic fowl of the smaller species.

The islands, scattered among these lakes, are neither so numerous nor so beautiful as might be accepted from the account. The remains of castles or religious edifices do not ornament them but they have their own reality. "There is a beautiful cluster on Winandermere; a pair pleasingly contrasted upon Rydal; nor must the solitary green island of Grasmere be forgotten. In the bosom of each of the lakes of Ennerdale and Devockwater is a single rock, which, owing to its neighbourhood to the sea, is: 'The haunt of coromorants and sea-mews' clang,' a music well suited to the stern and wild character of the several scenes!"[5] It is appropriate to mention here that above the surface of Derwent—water and other places, one may see a tract of spongy ground covered with aquatic plants. The lakes are fed by a multitude of brooks and torrents and internal springs, which circulate them like veins. Thus they are truly living lakes. The water is also pure and crystal clear. Besides these lakes, this region has some bodies of still water called Tarns. An unsightly tract of boggy ground often surrounds Tarns. They differ from a lake in being smaller and in belonging mostly to a smaller valley or circular recess. In fact, they are miniature lakes. Loughrigg Tarn, near Grasmere is the most beautiful example.

The most important rivers of this region are River Derwent and River Duddon. The water of these rivers is pellucid through which their beds of rock or of blue gravel may be seen in an exquisitely cerulean colour. In fact, their beauty is such and so various as is unequalled.

The description would be incomplete without describing the woods which are full of oak, ash, birch, wych elm—with underwood of hazel, the white and black thorn and hollies. Yews are found among the rocks. Alders and willows abound in moist places. As regards to weather, the rain here comes down heartily and is frequently succeeded by clear bright weather.

Vapours exhaling from the lakes and meadows after sun-rise, in a hot season, or in moist weather, brooding upon the heights, or descending towards the valleys with inaudible motion, give a visionary character to everything around them; . . . such clouds, cleaving to their stations or lifting up suddenly their glittering heads from behind rocky barriers, or hurrying out of sight with speed of the sharpest edge—will often tempt an inhabitant to congratulate himself on belonging to a country of mists and clouds and storms and make him think of the blank sky of Egypt, and of the cerulean vacancy of Italy, as an unanimated and even a sad spectacle.[6]

Thus the beauty of Lake District was beautiful enough to attract Wordsworth. The myriad aspects of various objects of Nature became so permanently fixed in his imagination that he couldn't think anything beyond Nature and went to the verge of spiritualizing Nature.

Lake District in Wordsworth's Poetry

It was the good fortune of England and English poetry that Wordsworth was born in the heart of an "unfenced region of society"—a region of green valleys, bleak moorlands, rugged mountains, lakes and streams, rocks and torrents. "An Evening Walk" was his first attempt to describe the Lake District and its influence upon him. Only this poem is sufficient to describe the beauty of the region and Wordsworth's intense love for his birth place. Wordsworth has described the region with such vividness and picturesqueness that one can't live without aspiring to have a sight of the same. The very opening of the poem presents marvellous scenery of the place:

Far from my dearest Friend, 't is mine to rove
Through bare gray dell, high wood, and pastoral cove;
His wizard course where hoary Derwent takes,
Through crags and forest glooms and opening lakes,

(An Evening Walk)

The poet as a boy was full of joy. The natural beauty and changing phases of this region affected the mind and spirit of the poet. He describes about an evening walk of this region. He starts with the description of the noon as the introductory part of evening. "Around the glaring hill" noon was "brooding still". There appeared shades of clouds. In such a natural surroundings, the poet wandered, hoping that the tomorrow's noon will again fill him with "wildwood strain". The sun declines. The landscape shines with a glow as the long rays and shades spread everywhere:

To mark the birches' stems all golden light,
That lit the dark slant woods with silvery white;

* * *

Their moveless boughs and leaves like threads of gold;
The skiffs with naked masts at anchor laid,

(An Evening Walk)

The life of this region is free from the din of cities. After finishing their work in the evening, potters, peasants, dalesmen, return to their cottages. Various groups of these workers can be seen "winding from side to side up the steep road". Sometimes they go to some lonesome chapel to ring the humble bells. Even the simplest part of this region is not undelightful. "The grassy door of mountain farms", "blue pomp of lakes", "high cliffs and falling floods", etc., all provide immense pleasure. The shepherd, directing his winding dog scales the cliffs. The radiance of the oaks that overhung the road, falls on "tawny earth". The oaks' darkening boughs and foliage twines may make the evening solemn but when one comes to the tranquil lake, a pleasant sight may be seen. One can visualize the swans "floating on the silvered waters glow". The swan with his towering wings is not alone. To grace the sight, there is

The female with a meeker charm succeeds,
And her brown little ones around her leads.
Nibbling the water-lilies as they pass,
Or playing wanton with the floating grass.

(An Evening Walk)

In such a surrounding, the song of mountain streams, which are not heard by day, can be heard by the poet. He is thrilled to hear the "aerial music of the hill".

Wordsworth's early life in Lake District and his later life in London and the course of French Revolution presents a "fundamental opposition which was developing in his experience between the simple benevolence of an organic Lakeland community and the life of an acquisitive and confused university society beyond; and return to Grasmere in December 1799 was a very important homecoming after many years of wandering."[7] The poem "Home at Grasmere" celebrates the value of Grasmere as "home". It is not a habitation only but in deeper sense the poet feels at peace with himself and at home with all his surroundings in ways, which he could never feel elsewhere.

The Prelude provides a graphic description of Lake District. The poet spent many years of his life in this region. In beautiful surrounding and congenial atmosphere of this region Wordsworth was born and brought up. Not only the physical aspects of the region but its influence upon the mind and spirit of the poet has also been described in detail. He describes the river Derwent as "the fairest of all rivers". The river is not a river, but "a tempting playmate whom we dearly loved". Derwent, after leaving the mountains and after receiving on its smooth surface the shadow of the towers of Cockermouth Castle, flows on along the side of the poet's terrace walk. The poet used to take a dive into the river and bask in the sun in turns throughout a summer's day. The river is not only physically beautiful, but it affects the poet's dreams also.

And, from his alder shades and rocky falls,
And from his fords and shallows, sent a voice
That flowed along my dream?

(*The Prelude* I, 272-74)

The poet used to enjoy the beauty of the rocks, hills, forests and fields of this region. He describes the mountain Skiddaw with its lofty height "bathed in the brilliant rays of the sun". It appeared "bronzed with deepest radiance". Born in Cockermouth, he shifted to Esthwaite "the beloved vale". He spent his school days at Hawkshead at the northwest end of this vale. Among the "sandy fields" were "flowery groves" of "yellow ragwort". In different seasons the place assumes different facets of beauty. In autumn, when the frost and chilly wind used to bite sharply, "Woodcocks ran/Among the green turf." In spring this cultivated valley was full of warmth and mother birds used to build their nests on high places. In summer, the poet used to gaze at the silver mist rising up in a curling manner or at the calm and smooth surface of lakes, seas and rivers darkened by over-hanging clouds. At that time, the poet's fancy took a new shape. Very often in the evening when the sea had cast off its gloomy shade of the evening and brightened up under the light of the rising moon, which was noticed and welcomed by the shepherds from their huts in distant hill, the poet used to stand and gaze at the scene. In fact he felt like sucking in beauty from the minutest part of the scene as a bee sucks in honey from the flowers.

The poet used to spend his summer over the surface of Lake Winandermere. At that time, the islands in the midst of the lake used to resound with the musical sounds of the birds. Some other island was full of shady oaks and was sown over with lilies of the valley. The poet mentions about the ruined church, which was there in the valley. Wordsworth used to go there during his visit to the country. This scene impressed the poet very much as he describes:

Some famed temple where of yore
The Druids worshipped, or the antique walls

Of that large abbey, where within the Vale
Of Nightshade, to St. Mary's honour built,
Stands yet a mouldering pile with fractured arch,
Belfry, and images, and living trees,
A holy scene!

(*The Prelude* II , 101-07)

Again he describes a public house (The White Lion) half way on the eastern bank of long Winander. This was not a plain type of building having a look of ancient simplicity like the cottages in the neighbourhood. It was a "splendid place". But this place was more beautiful before the hall was built on the large island (Belle Isle).

More worthy of a poet's love, a Hut
Proud of its own bright fire and sycamore shade

(*The Prelude* 147-48)

There are many more passages in *The Prelude* that give a pictorial delineation of the region. Wordsworth was not satisfied with the sensuous pleasures of the region but he found a new vision here hitherto undescribed by any poet. As a poet this is his most important contribution and herein lies his chief originality. He spiritualizes the moods of nature and wins from them moral consolation. In the beginning or as a boy his passion for Nature was nourished by his surroundings without any conscious or deliberate effort on his part—"By nourishment that came unsought". While wandering in various parts of the region, the poet

... drinking in a pure
Organic pleasure from the silver Wreaths
Of curling mist, or from the level plain
Of waters coloured by impending clouds.

(*The Prelude* I, 563-66)

The poet passed his time in exciting sports and pastimes. Soon he seemed to have a conscious urge to have Nature "collaterally attached" to all their plans for all sorts of games and pleasures. His boating excursions "over the shadowy lake" and riding adventures on "the galloping steed" over hills and dales, "through rough and smooth" brought the poet in closer contact with the charming and sublime aspects of nature. Slowly Wordsworth's sympathies or spiritual powers enlarged and familiar and common objects of Lake District became dearer to him day by day. He then began to love the sun not for its life-giving power but because it bathed the hills in its radiant beauty at dawn and touched the hills with its golden fingers before it set in the west.

Now the Lake District turned the poet and made him an immortal figure. His attachment to Nature grew into a religious love. He had mystic visions and had a feeling of the existence of a visionary power, a creative sensibility within himself and had a realization of the unity and harmony underlying all the diversities of Nature. The magic of the region is such that the poet is now gifted with a plastic power and hence:

. . . And auxiliary light
Came from mind, which on the setting sun
Bestowed new splendour: the melodious birds,
The fluttering breezes, fountains that run on
Murmuring so sweetly in themselves, obeyed
A like dominion and the midnight storm
Grew darker in the presence of my eye.

(The Prelude, II 368-740)

In fact it was the influence of this region that made him "the high priest of Nature". There may not be the direct description of the place, but its glimpses are scattered here and there through his poetry.

References

1. Wordsworth, William, *A Guide through the District of the Lakes*, London, Longman & Co., Maxon and Whittaker & Co. 1835, p. 173.

2. *Ibid.*, p. 174.

3. *Ibid.*, p. 176.

4. *Ibid.*, p. 181.

5. *Ibid.*, p. 184.

6. *Ibid.*, p. 191.

7. Watson, J.R., *English Poetry of the Romantic Period*, 1789-1830, Essex Longman Group Limited, p. 111.

7

Classical Myths

In all the periods of literature, the great literary figures have shown interest in dealing with myths. It has been a favourite tool for handling their central themes. The mythology had a distinct place in the literature of Renaissance and Romanticism. With the fall of Constantinople, the Greek treasures of Byzantine were scattered over the whole of Europe. Although the new learning reached England quite late yet it arrived at a time when the minds of men were ready to receive it. There runs a thread of classical mythology through all the Elizabethan literature. Romantic poets, who took inspiration from Elizabethan literature, were also attracted towards myths and mythology. In fact Romantic movement proclaimed a new birth of the mythological tradition.

Myths describe things so authoritatively that they transcend the ordinary reason and observation. They describe the origin or death of the world or the state of paradise; they describe a thing, which a man is not capable of seeing with his eyes. It explains social, natural or cultural facts. In the *Encyclopaedia Britannica* myth has been defined thus:

> *Myths are accounts with an absolute authority that is implied rather than stated, they relate events and states of affairs surpassing the ordinary human world, yet basis to that world; the time in which the related events take place is all together different from the historical time of human experience (and in most cases is unimaginably long ago) the actors in the narrative are usually gods or other extra-ordinary beings (such as animals, plants, the very first people, or specific men who changed the human conditions.*[1]

There are a number of theories about the origin of myths. According to most of them the myths, gods and many mythical personages are of a highly complex character and are composed of elements varying in origin as well as in their development, metamorphoses is worth mentioning. Myths were associated with astronomy. All the gods and goddesses were associated with the objects of nature, i.e., plants and trees, etc. Myths were taken as media to explain the geographical systems. Many myths have got their origin in the explanation of ritual practice.

Different scholars have defined and interpreted myths differently but the gist of all of them is that legends, tales, fables, etc., are the various forms of a myth. They fulfil various functions in literature. In Romantic era, the revitalization of myth followed two principal approaches— firstly, the symbolical interpretation of classical divinities and legendary figures and secondly, the interpretations of the great myths in the light of contemporary philosophical concepts, sometimes with a decided personal twist.

Wordsworth was one of the first great poets fully to possess himself of that myth of a transitional epoch by which we have been living through the industrial and technological revolutions. "His response to the myth was to hold tenaciously to personal and natural wisdom as against culture, and to a human and natural time-scale as against the measure of historical time."[2] Wordsworth was a voracious reader. He read many Classical and Elizabethan writers, while living in Cambridge. The Renaissance literature was saturated with the mythological references. Wordsworth could catch the spirit of the ancients. His Prelude and other poems are woven into mythical pattern. A study of them provides an interesting reading.

Wordsworth's poet is a mythological figure. Wordsworth has used the myth of Bible in describing his poet. The poet is revealed as made in the image of his maker. "The Vale in which the enfranchised and consecrated Poet of *The Prelude* is to live his holy life, the grove and sweet stream, the green fields, clouds and sky, the wild water on shore as he quits the tiresome sea, 'green herbs' and 'fruits fresh from their native bough', the vernal promises."[3] These constitute another Eden, in the prime tradition of Hebraic culture:

Thus long I mused
Nor e'er lost sight of what I mused upon,
Save when, amid the stately grove of oaks,
Now here, now there, an acron, from its cup
Dislodged, through sere leaves rustled, or at once
To the bare earth dropped with a startling sound.

(*The Prelude*, 80-85)

The Poet of Wordsworth is verily another Biblical Adam, man from the clay. "The earth is all before" the later it was all before the earlier man. Here in "one sweet Vale" his holy life is to be led; here in "one neighbourhood" ensuing days will bring admiration, love, "the life in common things", rare things in endless store; here he will find "self-congratulation, . . . complete composure, ... and put him in the garden of Eden to dress it and keep it". This and the command to replenish the earth and subdue it reappear in the Genesis of *The Prelude* as "a longing"

To brace myself to some determin'd aim,
Reading or thinking, either to lay up
New stores, or rescue from decay the old
By timely interference.

(*The Prelude* I, 115-8)

"Be fruitful, says the Book of Genesis. Wordsworth's Poet obediently hopes to 'endue,' to fix in a visible home' certain 'phantoms of conceit,' to deal forth temperately 'to such Beings' the feelings of his own heart. Taking a hint from the generation of Adam for his list of patriarchal heroes in the initial passage of *The Prelude* he gives us a 'little band of yet remembered names' which include old Britons 'left unsung' by Milton, Knight telling of Knight, shepherd piping of Shepherd, Mithridates becoming Odin, the friends and followers of Sertorious in the Fortunate Isles, the 'unknown man' unheard of in the Chronicles of Kings' but suffering in silence 'for the love of truth,' Dominique de Gourges, Gustavus of Sweden with his miners of Dalecarlia and Wallace, whose deeds, 'like a family of ghosts,' were left 'to people the steep rocks and river banks ... with a local soul of independence and stern liberty.'"[4]

"And a river went out of Eden to water the garden": and our poet presents an actual Derwent or the symbolic imagination:

We have traced the stream
From the blind cavern, whence is faintly heard
Its natal murmer;
* * *
And lastly, from its progress have we drawn

Faith in life endless, the sustaining thought
Of human Being, Eternity and God.

(*The Prelude* XIV, 194-205)

The poet cannot prove "false steward" in such a paradise and with such a divine commission and in such a lofty company. Adam was put into the Garden of Eden to dress it and keep it, but did neither. "Wordsworth associates his own vague longing, timorous capacity, infinite delay, subtle selfishness, false activity, with the old human error; his mind, too, turns "recreant" to her poetic task." This may be called another fall of man; the joyful "Sabbath" is over; the lofty hopes are to be yielded up "for present gifts of humbler industry". His Poet like Adam must get to work.

The Prelude can be interpreted in a different mythical way also. The pattern of *The Prelude* is that of an individual Paradise Lost. Wordsworth has conceived of the major process of his life as a myth; the child is in paradise and steps out of it into the turbulent world of the 1790s. He finds himself in the circumstances of the fallen world. We as human beings have to live in a world of struggle, of ideals that are thwarted, of confusion of mind, of societies that are life-denying and of political institutions that are corrupt. The young man's experience of this world is at once an unhappy one and also a necessary one: in his own life he encounters a "fall", but it is a fall from which he can, if preserved by the right spirit and temper, emerge stronger than before. Wordsworth therefore extends the first two parts of *The Prelude* into an epic, which in its own way parallels and enacts *Paradise Lost*. Wordsworth's description of the process of growing up as one of loss and gain is similar to Milton's description of the "fortunate fall". Adam and Eve go out into the world to make their own lives with their own choices:

The world was all before them, where to choose
Their place of rest, and providence their guide ...

(XII, 646-47)

Wordsworth echoes this in his own "glad preamble" to *The Prelude,* when he writes "The Earth is all before me" (I, 15)

With a heart
Joyous, nor scared at its own liberty,
I look about; and should the chosen guide
Be nothing better than a wandering cloud
I cannot miss my way.

(*The Prelude* I, 14-18)

Adam and Eve are guided by Providence but Wordsworth by a wandering cloud. Choice itself becomes a delight when the poet is surrounded by nature. Milton had asserted his right to make an epic out of Christian themes of patience and heroic martyrdom rather than out of heroes and battles; now Wordsworth asserts his right to make an epic out of the life of a child and young man in the 1770s, 1780s, and 1790s. Wordsworth presents the myth of the lost paradise in describing his childhood and youth. The subject is nothing less than becoming human as Adam and Eve become human after the fall.

The very process of writing *The Prelude* echoes the myth of *Samson Agonistes*. Wordsworth echoes Samson's first speech in which he wonders why special powers have been given to him if he is now lying captive in a Philistine gaol. Wordsworth feels like Samson, given great gifts, which he has failed to use. Coleridge, who wanted him to write The Recluse, was pressing him throughout this period "the first great philosophical poem". Wordsworth side-stepped this and turned aside to write what was to him far more important, an epic poem *The Prelude.*

As a nature poet, Wordsworth creates a nature myth not described by any poet as yet. Wordsworth thought Nature as a source of inspiration for virtuous life and a source of his own ecstasy. He created a myth about himself and built a philosophy about himself. The myth was this. He thought that in his younger days he was delighted with coarser pleasures and glad animal movement. These pleasures became less coarse in course of time. This was a period of aching joys and dizzy raptures. "Then the eye and ear started not only perceiving but half creating and the result was that blessed mood in which the motion of human blood seemed to be suspended and the poet seemed to be laid asleep in body and become a living soul."[5] In "Ode: Intimation of Immortality", Wordsworth supplements his myth of development by another idea. The idea is that childhood—including Wordsworth's own—was a period in which the spiritual beauty of the world was revealed to the human eye. He tried to induce himself to believe that the power of vision which was his in 1798—and was lost—was the common possession of all men in their childhood. The curse of man was that when he grew up, he became wicked and lost innocence. Wordsworth had "loved" nature neither in his childhood nor in his boyhood. Instead of dizzy raptures, he had felt terror in nature. He describes the feeling in the famous passage about the Cliff in *The Prelude,*

O'er my thoughts
There hung a darkness, call it solitude,
Or blank desertion. No familiar shapes
Remained, no pleasant images of trees,
Of sea or sky, no colours of green fields;
But huge and mighty forms, that do not live

Like living men mov'd, slowly through the mind
By day, and were a trouble to my dreams.

(*The Prelude* I, 393-400)

This fear of nature is expressed even in "Tintern Abbey" where the poet says that in his younger days he was:

More like a man
Flying from something that he dreads, than one
Who sought the thing he loved. (72-74)

In *The Prelude* Wordsworth seems to indicate that it was not only the solitary Cliff that filled his heart with fear for once; it was a frequent experience, which the Spirit of the Universe used for purifying the human soul:

Purifying thus
The elements of feeling and of thought,
And sanctifying, by such discipline,
Both pain and fear, until we recognize
A grandeur in the beatings of the heart.

(*The Prelude* I, 410-14)

Pain and fear were real; the dizzy raptures were a myth. In the second part of the myth, Wordsworth told himself and his readers that he was a different and superior being with the appearance of the blessed mood. In the eyes of his sister he sees a former pleasures; he wants to behold in her "what I was once". Like a sage he blesses the little one,

Let the moon
Shine on thee in thy solitary walk.

He hopes that her "wild ecstasies" after some time "shall be matured into a sober pleasure". Very soon Wordsworth was to find that the blessed mood had deserted even him. Thus the story of his own development as told by Wordsworth is not true. He was a man not essentially different from his sister. In tracing his development he was deluding himself about the permanence of the blessed mood. The only development in his attitude to nature seems to have been this. In his earlier years he had been either indifferent to nature or been afraid of it. In later years, with the help of the sister who gave him eyes and ears, he learnt to be more sensitive to the world around him. He sustained the myth that he could get more out of nature than most other people could. The critics followed him and treated him seriously as a "philosopher". In his mature stage he looks on Nature and hears in it

The still sad music of humanity,
Nor harsh nor grating, though of ample power
To chasten and subdue.

The dialectic of the senses here is vital in Wordsworth. The young child has an organic sense that combines seeing and hearing. The older child has some awakening to the phenomenal world. He sees a gleam in it that the mature man cannot see again. "But the man gains an intimation of immortality, of his renewed continuity with the young child, by hearing a still sad music as he sees a soberer colouring in Nature. Here in "Tintern Abbey", eight years before the completion of the Great Ode, Wordsworth anticipates the totality of its myth."[6]

In the book I of *The Excursion,* the wanderer is telling a story. Though he insists that he is telling a common tale, / An ordinary sorrow of man's life but the accents in which he begins his story mark his intention as prophetic:

Thus did he speak, 'I see around me here
Things which you cannot see: we die, my friend,
Nor we alone, but that which each man loved

And prized in his peculiar nook of earth
Dies with him, or is changed; and very soon
Even of the good is no memorial left.

(*The Excursion* I, 469-74)

The poet presents the burden of the story in a mythical manner. A family disintegrates; the wife, Margaret, abandoned by her husband, gradually loses hope of his return, allowed one of her children to leave her for a distant farm, the other to fall ill and die. She herself finally dies and her cottage and its garden are now to be seen in the slow process of wasting back into the landscape. Like Milton's story of the Flood, the story of Margaret may be taken as an object lesson: the dead child, the overgrown garden, the ruined cottage speak of the same losses that Adam is made to feel when he learns that the flood will sweep away his descendents and his dwelling place. The dialogue of Adam and Archangel is recapitulated by the understanding of the Wanderer. "There is even a Wordsworthian analogue of the redemptive process, for it is suggested that Nature herself, the Nature that ministered to the Wanderer as a child, is providentially overseeing this episode in human history."[7]

Myth of Laodameia

Inspired by the direct observation of Nature Wordsworth's imagination took the course of classical myths to express him in a forceful manner. Laodameia is not a poem written on the fable of Laodameia. It is an expression of the ideas by which Wordsworth wanted to emphasis the importance of spiritual love. The chief inspiration behind Laodameia was Virgil. Laodameia is one of the unhappy lovers in *Aeneid,* book VI. In this poem Wordsworth expresses with classical elegance and firmness a stoic view of human passion. It is based on classical myth and elaborated in the classical manner. Wordsworth himself wrote about the poem: "The incidents of the trees growing and withering put the subject into my thoughts, and I wrote with the hope of giving it a loftier tone than, so far as I know, has been given to it by any of the ancients who have treated of it. It has cost me more trouble than almost anything of equal length I have ever written."

In fact, the poet's aim in writing this poem was to lend a charm of loftiness and grandeur to an ancient theme, which had not been so treated by any of the earlier poets. The subject is Virgilian, and so is the style, or it is an English adaptation of the Virgilian style, or it is an English adaptation of the Virgilian style, reminding us now of Milton, now of Pope. It achieves a noble ease and dignity with smoothly moulded phrases and many echoes of the Greek and Latin poets.

Laodameia was the wife of Protesilaus and the daughter of Acastus, king of Locus. Protesilaus, a native of Phylace of Thessaly, was slain by the Trojan prince Hector as per prophecy of the oracle of Apollo at Delphi that the first Greek to land on the Trojan sea-shore will be instantly killed. After her husband's death, Laodameia begged the gods to restore him to life and allow her to converse with him. The gods granted her request. Hermes (Mercury) brought Protesilaus back to the upper world for three hours.

After three hours he died a second time. Laodameia could not bear the separation and she too died with her husband. According to classical legend, from the tomb of Protesilaus, for whom Laodameia died, there grew for ages a group of lofty trees. As soon as they reached the height from which the walls of Troy were visible, they withered but again they grew till that height. There was continual growing and withering.

Here, Wordsworth expresses with classical elegance and firmness a stoic view of human passion. Wordsworth lays emphasis on the devotion to duty. He suggests that sensual delights and sexual pleasures should be discarded in favour of temperance and self-control. The joys of senses vanish very soon and the earth destroys physical raptures. Only calm pleasures and majestic pains abide. Protesilaus, in fact, speaks for Wordsworth:

Be taught, O faithful consort, to control
Rebellious passion: for the Gods Approve
The depth, and not the tumult of the soul;
A fervent, not ungovernable, love. (73-76)

Love should not be an expression of mere sensuality. It should remain under the control of reason and duty. Laodameia is condemned, for she is, strong in love "but too weak in reason" and "too slow in self government". Love does not aim at trivialities:

Learn by a mortal yearning, to ascend-
Seeking a higher object, love was given,
Encouraged, sanctioned, chiefly for that end.

The stoic view imparts a lofty tone. The overpowering passion of Laodameia would have thrilled Shelley, Byron or Browning. But it could not please Wordsworth, the moralist. For her overpowering passion, Laodameia is admonished and punished. W.A. Heard presents the moral ideas in the poem:

"The idea that underlies the poem is the same conception of 'piety' which Virgil has embodied in the Aeneid. 'Piety' embraces all the duties of life that are based upon the affection—love of home and parents and children, love of the gods of our fathers and a reverence for that order of things in which man finds a part. The pious man believes in a destiny or other power transcending his own will: to

exalt any passion, however innocent, is a rebellion; to intensify any passion, so as to disturb the appropriate calm of resignation, is to act irreverently against the gods. Lesser duties must give way to greater; love of wife give way to love of country and the sorrow of bereavement must not obscure the larger issues of life. Thus, not only did Laodameia's yearnings for the restoration of her husband to life show a failure to recognize the fixity of eternal laws, but her death was a transgression of the ordinance of destiny and in reason's spite; it was, after all, self-will and could not find favour of heaven."[8]

Thus the poet has shown love in conflict with reason and duty. Love is given to mortals, encouraged, sanctioned for the lofty purpose of ascending towards a higher object. The lesson to be learnt from the poem is summed in the following lines:

The gods approve
The depth, and not the tumult of the soul
A fervent, not ungovernable love.

Thus the myth in the poetry of Wordsworth is the media for the exploration of poetic resources. They provide him a process, a movement, psychologically speaking, from conscious to unconscious and again to the heightened consciousness. The poet enlarges his individual consciousness to the collective consciousness of myth, a collective consciousness of men from age to age.

Their Relevance

Myths are natural expressions of reality. They are not contrived or artificial, but reflections of eternal truth that transcends appearances. They draw on matters of common knowledge, on events which are familiar to their audience and their time. For this reason their message is always accessible to those who are alert and receptive in all ages and in all places. They are the natural possession of the human soul and the inspiration of the human mind. We find in every continent on earth carvings, monuments, engravings, symbolic pictograms, statuary—every kind of quasi-permanent record that can convey ideas and supply information on the most vital concerns of human life. What is most striking about them is that the ideas they contain are remarkably similar everywhere. However widely separated in time and place, however much they differ in language and cultural form, they all feature certain key thoughts. These key ideas deal with the origin of life, the purpose of living and the goal of evolution, particularly human evolution.

Myths include everything, at least in principle. In it, we find spiritual truth, logical philosophy, even scientific facts. Many of its stories allude to things that have only lately been discovered in nuclear physics and chemistry at one end of the spectrum; and at the other they refer to divine powers that ensoul the stars in space. If we can decipher the symbolic code of myths and look honestly at the factual content, we may find that science is just now beginning to catch up with what may be the most complete natural science in the world. It is surely the oldest natural science in the world, the one which has been available all along in many forms of mythology, but which has been consistently ignored.

It seems strange that what prevents myths from being taken seriously today is the very fact that they point to truths only recently learned by our most learned skilled researchers. We consider that modern man is at the top of the line of evolution, so we don't believe that anything miraculous could possibly have been known before our kind of technology came into picture. Mythic science is therefore dismissed. While we spend time and squander resources battering in the physicals of the temple of learning, the keys may lie unsuspected in the wells of wisdom which surround us on all sides.

In its own way every mythology describes the compassionate act of the gods who kindled our ability to think, to choose and to pursue our human destiny with full awareness. The first human thinkers had to learn who they were and what their function was to be in the world. They were taught the sciences of physical survival. They were even imbued with something of the gods' own wisdom and direct cognition of divine law. Indeed what the gods taught the first human beings still remains with us as innate recognition of truth. In human beings, evolution is a matter of mental enlightenment and spiritual growth. It is patently impossible for any growth of consciousness to take place unless it can build on previously acquired faculties and skills accumulated by experience.

In the late 18th century, the role of the emotions was emphasized and correspondingly, to play down the importance of reason. Those involved in the new movements were known as Romantics. The Romantic Movement had profound implications for the study of myth. Myths in the form of stories from Greek and Roman antiquity and contemporary folktales were regarded by the Romantics as repositories of experience. They were regarded more vital and powerful than the artificial art and poetry of the aristocratic civilization of contemporary Europe. Wordsworth applied various figures of Greek and Roman mythology to preach the people of his time. As we see in the sonnet "The World is too much with Us":

Great God ! I'd rather be
A Pagan suckled in a creed outworn;

So might I standing on this pleasant lea,
Have glimpses that would make me less forlorn;
Have sight of Proteus rising from the sea;
Or hear old Triton blow his wreathed horn.

A person can be destroyed only if he is taken away from his roots. No one can be destroyed as long as he is rooted deep into the soil of his motherland to the native bond. Wordsworth has immortalized his native region through poetry. Lake District occupies an important place in the pages of English literature. If we want to know about this region, we should go through the poetry of Wordsworth and we will know everything about it.

References

1. Benton, William, *The New Encyclopaedia Britannica,* Chicago, the University of Chicago, Founded 1768, 15th ed., p. 194
2. Sharrock, Roger, "The Prelude: the Poet's Journey to the Interior", *English,* Vol. XIX Spring 1970, number 103, p. 2.
3. C.F. Genesis I, 9-11 and I, 30, "every green herb". Milton says (*Paradise Lost* VII, 336-7): "every herb ... on the green stemm." Quoted in Abbie Findlay Potts, *Wordsworth's Prelude: A Study of Its Literary Forms,* New York Cornell University Press, 1953, p. 340.
4. Potts, Abbie Findlay, *Wordsworth's Prelude: A Study of Its Form,* p. 341.
5. Sharma, Ram Bilas, *Studies in Nineteenth Century English Poetry,* Pustak Bhawan, Agra, 1961, p. 8.
6. Bloom, Harold, "The Myth of Memory and Natural Man", quoted in *Wordsworth: A Collection of Critical*

Essays (ed.), M.H. Abrams, New Delhi, Prentice Hall of India Limited, p. 98.

7 Hertz, Neil, "Wordsworth and The Tears of Adam", quoted in *Wordsworth: A Collection of Critical Essays* (ed.), M.H. Abrams, p. 121.

8. Heardm, W.A., quoted in K.N. Khandelwal, *William Wordsworth: Selected Poems*, Agra, Laxmi Narain Agrawal, Educational Publishers, p. 184.

8

Nature and Man in Wordsworth

Shakespeare, Milton, and Wordsworth are the three great mountain ranges of almost equal height, other poets are only peaks and up of many poets. To ascend Wordsworth is to ascend a mountain around which there clings a perpetual mist. Often that mist is blown apart or disappears and then landscapes open below us. These are the landscapes of the mind of men comparable to those we see in Milton and Shakespeare. And then the mist gathers again and we are for a while lost in it. It is this mist and mystery gathering over the reality, this intermission of sight, which is unique in Wordsworth. The manner in which Shakespeare, Milton and Wordsworth respectively move us, is a subject for another inquiry. Roughly, Shakespeare does it mostly by a unison of many implied intellectual as well as emotional intensities; Milton does it by arousing a sense of the awful spiritual importance of a particular intensity and Wordsworth by arousing a sense of the unity of individual life with universal life.

Wordsworth's view of Nature is well known. He had a new and original philosophy to unfold, a new and individual view of Nature to expound.. He is concerned far less with the sensuous manifestations that delight most of the poets of Nature, than with the spiritual. His view of nature is different from that of other poets of his age. His love of Nature developed through various stages. His childhood days were spent in the midst of beautiful sights and sounds of Nature. Wordsworth's first love of Nature was a healthy boy's delight in outdoor life. In the second stage, Wordsworth developed a passion for the sensuous beauty of Nature. As he grew up, his "coarser pleasures" lost their charm for him. He loved Nature with an unreflecting passion altogether untouched by intellectual interests or associations. All these aching joys and dizzy raptures came to an end with his experiences of human suffering in France. The French Revolution opened his eyes and made him realize the dignity of the common man. In the third stage his love of Nature became linked with the love of man. Now he could hear in Nature, "The still sad music of humanity". This stage was soon followed by the final stage of the spiritual interpretation of Nature. After his "merciless ravage", something mysterious touched him, and he felt that "there is a spirit in the woods". From now onwards he realized a divine principle reigning in the heart of Nature. This is known as the stage of Pantheism.

Mr. Wordsworth's genius is a pure emanation of the Spirit of the Age. He takes the simplest elements of Nature and of the human mind, the mere abstract conditions inseparable from our being and tries to compound a new system of poetry from them and has perhaps succeeded as well as any one could. His poetry is founded on setting an opposition between the natural and the artificial, between the spirit of humanity and the spirit of fashion and of the world. Wordsworth's concept of Nature and Man is to trace the action of his unique incommunicable faculty, that strange, mystical sense of a life in natural things and of man's life as a part of natural things, drawing strength and colour and character from local influences, from the hills and streams and from natural sights and sounds. This is the active principle in Wordsworth's poetry. As we find in "Micheal" where this sense of the beneficial interaction of Man and Nature is projected in the portrait of Michael himself, formed and strengthened by his mountainous environment and his enduring and durable will. Another milder and lesser rugged instance can be given of Lucy poems. In the poem "Three Years She Grew," he says:

The stars of midnight shall be dear
To her: and she shall lean her ear
In many a secret place
Where rivulets dance their wayward round
And beauty form of murmuring sound
Shall pass into her face.

The last two lines emphatically belong to Wordsworth and display the essential quality and character of his mind at its best. Wordsworth writes about Nature in contexts of his own beliefs an experience. He does so in his consciousness of the prophetic role. When he describes nature in "Tintern Abbey" as

The nurse
the guides, the guardian of my heart and soul
of my moral being...

(II, 109-11)

It should not be understood superficially. He is using precise language, which he wishes as prophet to declare to the world. In contrast to the mechanical diseased waste of life that is encouraged by modern urban society, there are ways of living that allows the fuller development of mind and heart:

Knowing that Nature never did betray
The heart that loved her: 'tis her privilege
Through all the years of this our life to lead
From joy to joy.

(Tintern Abbey II, 122-34)

Here Wordsworth seems to be a critic of society like Blabe and Byron, seeing a need for a radical change of heart, a complete rejection of contemporary assumptions and habits of thought. It is the sheer waste and sadness of life that angers him. He declares:

The world is too much with us late and soon
Getting and spending, we lay waste our powers
Little we see in Nature that is ours,
We have given our hearts away, a sordid boon.

(Miscellaneous Sonnets, XXXIII)

In this manner, the doctrine of nature in Wordsworth's poetry is an unremitting campaign against the destruction of the individual by material and social pressures. For this purpose, he described the poet as the rock of defence for human nature an upholder and preserver carrying everywhere with him relationship and love. He saw himself and Coleridge as prophets of Nature demonstrating the power and beauty of the mind of Man when influenced by Nature:

Prophets of Nature, we to them will speak
A lasting inspiration, sanctified
By reason and by truth; what we have loved
Others will love and we may teach them how
A thousand times more beautiful than the earth
On which he dwells.

(*The Prelude* XIII, 442-48)

Wordsworth seems to express the native and naked dignity of man and also the world seen "in the spirit of love". Some of the Lyrical Ballads like "Simon Lee", "Goody Blake and Harry Gill", "The Idiot Boy" are patently concerned with a native and naked dignity while others like 'Tintern Abbey' are involved with the world seen in a spirit of love. The finest of Wordsworth's Nature poetry explores the relationship between these two great themes and demonstrates the power of nature in the rescuing of the individual mind from degradation, materialism, selfishness and despair.

Wordsworth's two great preoccupations, the predicament of human life and the beauty of the natural world are demonstrated in his early poetry but in 'An Evening Walk' and "Descriptive Sketches", the two things are held in the same poem without any attempt at integration. Let us analyse "An Evening Walk"—written at school and during the Cambridge vacations, the poem describes the Lake District in the tradition of picturesque landscape, interrupted by the terrible portrayal of the soldier's widow and her two starving children. Her husband has been killed in the American War of Independence and she is left destitute, yet after the description of the death of her children, Wordsworth turns back to the twilight landscape without a flicker of hesitation:

Sweets are the sounds that mingle from afar
Heard by calm lakes as peeps the folding star.

His experiences as a solitary wanderer not only gave him the intense feeling towards Nature that is described in *Lyrical Ballads* but it also may have increased his identification with the poor and houseless. *Lyrical Ballads* is seen as a landmark in English Romantic poetry. Coleridge described its genesis in *Biographia Literaria:*

> *During the first year that Mr. Wordsworth and I were neighbours, our conservations turned frequently on the two cardinal points of poetry, the power of exciting the sympathy of the reader by a faithful adherence to the truth of Nature and the power of giving the interest of novelty by the modifying colours of imagination. The sudden charm, which accidents of light and shade, which moon light or sun-set diffuse over a known and familiar landscape, appeared to represent the practicability of combining both. These are the poetry of nature.*[1]

Truth and imagination, the transformation of reality, these are to be aims of the volume. Coleridge was to direct his attention "to persons an characters supernatural, or at least romantic". Wordsworth "was to propose to himself as his object to give the charms of novelty to things of every day."[2]

As the focus of this article is Nature and Man in Wordsworth, let me tell you that a number of poems in *Lyrical Ballads* present memorable figures. Goody Blake is an old poor woman gathering sticks from a hedge, the old shepherd has one lamb from his flock, having been forced to sell the others to feed his children. Martha Ray in "The Thorn" has been seduced, betrayed, has lost her child. These are all pitiable and memorable figures and their situations reflect the fundamental problems of human nature. In publishing them, Wordsworth was appealing over the heads of connoisseurs and poetasters to the fundamental sympathies of human heart. Here he is "a man speaking to men" as he makes clear in a letter written to John Wilson.

> *I answer, human nature, as it has been and ever will be. But where are we to find the best measure of this? I answer, from within, by stripping our own hearts naked, and by looking out of ourselves towards men who lead the simplest lines most according*

to nature; men who have never known false refinements—wayward and artificial desires, false criticisms, effeminate habits of thinking and feeling or who, having known these things have outgrown them.[3]

'The Idiot Boy' was the cause of this fine statement as Wilson did not like the poem and wrote a letter to Wordsworth, but in fact this poem is a very interesting example of Wordsworth's ability to transform and apparently unpromising subject into a great poem. *Lyrical Ballads* present a new type of subject matter and treatment radically new to the reader and unknown to the hundreds of contemporary examples. The relationship between human beings and the external world is the subject of the poem from *Lyrical Ballads* but the greatest celebration in *Lyrical Ballads* of the watching and receiving heart is the final poem "Tintern Abbey". In this poem, Wordsworth explores the effects of memory, time and landscape itself upon the human heart. The poem does not lose sight of the scene entirely and returns to it with a delightful allusion at the end, but it also records with great sensitivity and passion, the developing power of a mind and heart that are affected by Nature. The movement of the verse here is in three parts, each depending on the introductory two and a half lines. The first part signifies the blessed mood and the second shows a graceful diminuendo in the simple description of the inward eye succeeded by the simple daring totality of "We see into the life of things". This follows on from the climax of the passage when we 'become a living soul'. Thus one begins "A Presence", the second "a sense sublime" and the third "a motion and a spirit".

And I have felt
A presence that disturbs me with the joy
Of elevate thought; a sense sublime
Of something far more deeply interfuses

whose dwelling is the light of setting sun
and the round ocean and the living air
And the blue sky and in the Mind of Man
A motion and a spirit, that impels
All thinking things, all objects of al thought
And rolls through all things.

(Tintern Abbey)

The way in which "Tintern Abbey" moves from such moments of vision to the commonplace of human affection for the landscape is sure-footed and essential to the poem's effect. The use of words such as "blessings", "blessed", "genial" "sweet", "delightful", "joy" is an utterance of joy and celebration. The poet is reflecting on his good fortune in being present before the same beautiful landscape, which he remembered from the previous visit. In 1793, he had been

More like a man
Flying from something that he dreads than one
Who sought the thing he love one.
Now he finds a new maturity accompanied by the sense of—
The still, sad music of humanity
Nor harsh nor grating, though of ample power
To chasten and subdue.

(II, 91-95)

His enthusiasm for nature is no longer the frantic escape of 1793 when he was bewildered and shocked by the war, the progress of the revolution and the separation from Annette, now in 1798 he is recording his gratitude for his survival as a poet and his sense of the value of nature in relation to human life. Now he dwells on the mysterious presence of surrounding things. He always grasps the whole of nature as involved in the tonality of the particular instance. That is why he laughs with daffodils and finds in the primrose thoughts too deep for tears. Wordsworth's greatest poem is by far the first book of *The Prelude.* It is pervaded by this sense of the haunting presences of Nature. A series of magnificent passages, too long for quotation expresses this idea. Let us see an instance:

> *Ye presence of Nature in the sky*
> *And on the earth! Ye visions of the hills*
> *And souls of lonely places.*

Whatever may be his vision of Nature, he has dwelt among pastoral scenes till each object has become connected with a thousand feeling, a link in the chain of thought, a fibre of his own heart. Hazlitt's remark is worth seeing in this connection:

> *There is a lofty philosophic tone, a thoughtful humanity infused into his pastoral vein. Remote from the passions and events of the great world, he has communicated interest and dignity to the primal movements of the hearts of man and ingrafted his own conscious reflections on the casual thoughts of hinds and shepherds.*[4]

Wordsworth had two fundamental beliefs in the divinity of nature and the belief in the grandeur and dignity of man. The blend of these two closely related beliefs resulted in this typical celebration of figures like the Leech Gatherer, Michael or Nature's lady beings whose humanity is ennobled by close association with "mute insensate things". Many and great changes have taken place since Wordsworth's time. Few now have any faith in Nature or in Man or in the bond between Man and Nature. Yet as he is the first so he remains the type of the modern poets.

For Wordsworth, Nature is a living entity. The indwelling spirit of Nature imparts its own consciousness to all objects of Nature. If we explore the inner life of Nature as Wordsworth conceives it, we find that one of its characteristics is its joy. Wordsworth found Nature "kind" and "kindly" and it is "fostering Nature", "holy Nature". Nature teaches a "lesson deep of love". Wordsworth found in the meadows and the woods and mountains the spiritual stimulus that Blake sought in purely imaginary visions. As the more comprehensive poet, Wordsworth wanted to go beyond but not away from Nature. He remained a poet of "the mighty world of eye and ear" till the end of his life.

Nature is taken as a norm of conduct for Man. Science impartially notes that Nature is full of pleasure and pain, but Wordsworth regards Nature as "Fostering" mother, which leads birds to function as birds. Seizing on this hopeful aspect of things, Wordsworth reminds Man that he is capable of pleasure in a high degree and exhorts him to cultivate to the utmost the capacities with which Nature has endowed him. Wordsworth's love of Nature led him to love of Man. The French Revolution taught Wordsworth that every human being was intrinsically great and capable of infinite development. It promised to translate the idea into fact, and in the event disastrously belied its promise. But the poet did not give up his hopes for Man till he had tested human nature in its elements. How was this to be done? "By stripping our own hearts naked, and by looking out of ourselves towards men who lead the simplest lives, and those most according to Nature, men who have never known false refinements, wayward and artificial desires, effeminate way of thinking and feeling."[5] In his wanderings on the country roads he came in contact with the humblest human beings. Their strength and energy surprised him. He saw into the depths of human souls. Souls that appear to have no depth at all to careless eyes. In his poetry Wordsworth shows how human beings fit into the midst of the interplaying forces of Nature. In "Three Years She Grew in Sun and Shower", Lucy is taken up into the life of Nature and incorporated with it. The same is true of Michael, the Leech-gatherer, the Solitary Reaper, the Highland Girl, the Danish Boy, and Louisa in the Shade. Wordsworth believes that there is a pre-existing harmony between the mind of Man and Nature. "Man and Nature, Mind and the external world, are geared together and in unison complete the motive principle of the universe. They act and react upon each other, 'so as to produce an infinite complexity of pain and pleasure'. The exquisite functioning of this interlocked universe of Mind and Nature is for Wordsworth the highest theme of poetry; in poetry the process actually receives its final consummation."[6]

Since the individual mind and the external world are exquisitely fitted to each other, communion between the two is possible. But this communion is possible only when the soul of Man is in harmony with the soul of Nature. In his poetry Wordsworth shows how human beings, who are separated from all that in every day humanity is disturbing or distressing, take on something of "the silence and the calm / Of mute insensate things". In any attempt to understand what Nature meant to Wordsworth, due weight should be given to the healing power of the impersonal over a sick mind. It was when the "fretful stir Unprofitable, and the fever of the world" had long "hung upon the beatings of my heart" that he turned to Nature, and found "for this uneasy heart of ours a never-failing principle of joy". Up to the end, Wordsworth depicted Man amid impersonal influences, which glorify him and reduce the intensity of his sufferings and struggles. He believed that human beings were intrinsically great and capable of infinite development. Therefore he showed his reverence "to men as they are men within themselves". A careful reading of *The Prelude* clearly shows that Wordsworth received the best part of his education from Nature. In the first two books of this autobiographical poem we find that Nature has been acting as a sort of glorified parent or school-mistress.

Wordsworth's chief originality is, of course, to be sought in his poetry of Nature. What gives him his uniqueness is the fact that he is, of all English poets, the one who has given the most impressive and the most emotionally satisfying account of Man's relation to Nature. He is the greatest Nature poet of England because he is the poet of more than external Nature; he is, in a higher degree, the poet of Man. Many and great changes have taken place since Wordsworth's time. Few now have any faith in Nature or in Man or in the bond between man and nature. Yet as he is the first so he remains the type of the modern poets.

References

1. Coleridge, *Biographia Literaria* (ed.), James Engell and W.T. Bate London, II 5, Ch. XIV, 1983.
2. *Biographia Literaria*, II, 6-7, Ch. XIV.
3. Wordsworth to John Wilson, 7 June 1802; *The Letters of William and Dorothy Wordsworth, The Early Years 1787-1805*, Revised by Chester L. Shauer, Second Edition, Oxford, 1967, p. 355.
4. Hazlitt, William, *Lectures on English Poets: The Spirit of the Age*, New York, 1910, p. 255.
5. *The Early Letters of William and Dorothy Wordsworth*, Oxford University Press, London, 1935, p. 295.
6. Read, Herbert, *Wordsworth*, Faber & Faber Ltd., London, 1949, pp. 126-27.

9

Earth, Spade and Storm

Earth

In *Prelude* I, Wordsworth describes the earth in his own way. He has a belief that all Nature is alive with a spirit or soul of its own. When he goes out for skating in winter season, he feels that the earth seems to him to be moving about on its daily round in a palpable visible manner. The movement becomes slower and then stops but it makes the poet feel that there is some mysterious power at work in Nature. Sometimes he describes the motionless aspect of the earth:

All else was still;
No living thing appeared in earth or air.

(*The Prelude* IV, 384-85)

Wordsworth also describes the scene when the earth and the sky rang with the still glad music of humanity.

In "Ode on the Intimation of Immortality", the poet makes no distinction between Nature and the Earth. For Wordsworth, they are to be distinguished. The earth abounds with earthly pleasures as opposed to heavenly glories. The earth is compared with a foster mother. Man is taken away from his true, home namely, heaven and left in care of the foster mother, earth. Stanza VI, presents the earth, a homely buxom foster-mother to the princely soul that has come by way of Nature to her farm. She represents the benignly mindless peasant woman of pastoral romances who rears the foundling prince as best she can. She provides the new-born child with all kinds of pleasure to amuse him and make him forget his heavenly home.

Earth fills her lap with pleasures of her own:
Yearnings she hath in her own natural kind,
And, even, with something of a Mother's mind,
And, no unworthy aim,
The homely Nurse doth all she can
To make her foster child, her inmate Man,
Forget the glories he hath known,
And that imperial palace whence he came.

(The Immortality Ode, Stanza VI)

In Stanza VII, the infant who bears within him the wisdom to "sport upon the shore", is taught by his earthly parents to act the game of life, to store, until the adult's ordinary responses to a seemingly dead objective world become natural to him. This motherly affection can be seen in the fact that Wordsworth does not understand any human being as the burden of the earth as we see about the Cumberland beggar.

"At times Wordsworth's personification of external nature merges with, or is expressed in a way that suggests, belief in Mother Earth, the earth goddess Hertha, or the anima mundi: 'Listening to notes that are the ghostly language of the ancient earth'; 'the antiquated Earth beat like the heart of Man'; 'Love . . . is

stealing, from earth to man, from man to earth'; 'The human Soul of universal earth'".[1]

Wordsworth often presents the earth unified with the sky. The range of his seeing which describes in detail about the earth includes the hemisphere of the heaven as well. A joining of the earth and the sky was hardly a new action for Wordsworth. He presents this universal scheme of things in several poems. In "Tintern Abbey", the earth and the sky come together to show that what he sees does not stand alone in "absolute independent singleness" but stands as part of the wholeness which is the universe:

Once again
Do I behold these steep and lofty cliffs,
That on a wild secluded scene impress
Thoughts of more deep seclusion; and connect
The landscape with the quiet of the sky.

The poem "Night-Piece" shows similarity to the lyric on daffodils, particularly in its awareness of how earth and sky, in certain situations, have to be perceived together. Here he brings them into relationship through dullness and gloominess. He shows what they are not doing but soon will be when the moon breaks through:

The moon,
Which through that veil is indistinctly seen,
A dull, contracted circle, yielding light
So feebly spread that not a shadow falls,
Chequering the ground—from rock, plant, tree or tower.

Again in *The Prelude* II, Wordsworth has described a childhood experience which shows heaven and earth united in one:

Oh, then, the calm
And dead still water lay upon my mind

Even with a weight of pleasure, and the sky,
Never before so beautiful, sank down
Into my heart, and held me like a dream!

Wordsworth offers his own particular version of the holy marriage, the coming together of the sky and the earth. Whatever form this union may took, it always promises fruitfulness. In the above-mentioned passage quoted from *The Prelude,* water substitutes for earth. In the poem, "The Thorn", the earth is in the form of a mound where Martha goes to express the great pain of her heart. The mound is a "fresh sight". It is covered with lovely tints:

Of olive green and scarlet bright,
In spikes, in branches, and in stars,
Green, red, and pearly white!
This heap of earth o'ergrown with moss,
Which close beside the Thorn you see,
So fresh in all its beauteous dyes,

(The Thorn)

In midst of this luxuriant aspect of the earth, "An infant's grave" suddenly recalls the gloomy atmosphere. In fact, the colourful loveliness of the mound is in sharp contrast to the dereliction of the thorn. This beauteous piece of the earth is an image of natural beauty, joy and luxuriance. It is suggestive of innocence, while the thorn and the pond are connected with the world of experience of suffering and endurance.

Wordsworth suffers to be a resident of London. He does not like the hustle and bustle of cities. When he returns home, he feels immense pleasure. As he says in the beginning of *The Prelude* I: The earth is before me. The earth is synonymous to nature. He loves the earth for its mountain, meadows, woods and other beautiful objects.

Therefore am I still
A lover of the meadows and the woods
And mountains; and of all that we behold
From this green earth.

He also feels a "spirit" in the earth. Wordsworth describes the scientific fact about the earth, as the earth rotates on its axis. Lucy is brought up by mother earth. When she is no more, she is "rolled round" with the earth in its daily rotation. She is like a stone or rock or tree that can be "rolled" as the earth, while turning on its axis, is itself "rolled round" the sun.

At the political conditions, Wordsworth is sorry, so he feels that mother earth will also be in deep stress. In the poem "Invocation to the Earth", he describes the agony of the earth, which she feels at the violence, blood shedding and political chaos:

'Rest, rest, perturbed Earth!
O rest, thou doleful Mother of Mankind!
A Spirit sang in tones more plainative than the wind:
'From regions where no evil thing has birth
I come – thy stains to wash away,
Thy cherished fetters to unbind,
And open thy sad eyes upon a milder day.

Thus, earth plays an important part in the poetry of Wordsworth.

Spade

In such a large area of poetry Wordsworth has written a single poem about spade, "To a Spade of a Friend". He has a great honour for spade, as it is used to till the land, "Thou art a tool of honour in my hands". He likes to press it with pride when it yields the soil. This is an important tool for human beings, as it has always served man, "Long has thou served a man to reason true". Even if a man has to toil through the day, he will not dread. Not only an agriculturist but the whole species of human beings is benefited by it, "The labouring many, and resting few". A grave can't be dug without a spade, so the spade is greater than a trophy. It is a source of happiness and a way to reach the truth:

That man will have a trophy, humble spade!
A trophy nobler than a conquerer's sword.
If he be one that feels, with skill to part
False praise from true, or, greater from the less,
Thou will be welcome to his hand and heart,
Thou monument of peaceful happiness.

(*Poetical Works*, 383-84)

The reference of digging grave also appears in the poem "The Thorn". People wanted to dig out the body of Martha's baby from the grave, so they went there with their spades. Due to a natural miracle, the spades could not be used.

Spade is not simply an instrument. It also refers to work, specially manual labour. Wordsoworth may not have described spade directly in other poems but he has a great respect for manual labour. We are familiar with Michael, The Leech Gatherers and others who were very laborious. They are Wordsworth's favourite figures. A strikingly original response in Wordsworth to his shepherds is the acknowledgement that they worked. They were inhabitants of a world where work was of central importance:

Often times
When others heeded not, He heard the South
Make subterraneous music, like the noise

Of bagpipers on distant Highland hills.
The Shepherd, at such warning, of his flock
Bethought him, and he to himself would say,
'The winds are now devising work for me!'

(Michael, 49-55)

Wordsworth's acceptance of work is certainly one of the archaic validities in his view of things. He was natively habituated to the producer's rather than the consumer's attitude. Michael's whole life has been work:

Our lot is a hard lot: the sun himself
Has scarcely been more delight ......

All the members of his family were so hardworking that they had earned an almost proverbial reputation for their incessant work. It is fitting that the ending of Luke's stay with his father should be celebrated by the beginning of a new work of building and care:

Now fare thee well-
When thou return'st , thou in this place will see
A work which is not here: a covenant
Twill be between us; but, whatever fate
Befall thee, I shall love thee to the last.

(Michael, 412-16)

The Solitary Reaper is also alone in her work. "Leech Gatherer" is also a working man doing "Employment, hazardous and weariness". He tells Wordsworth that he earns his livelihood by roaming the moors and gathering leeches from ponds. The poet is amazed to see the old man's indomitable, majestic soul, cheerful indifference to difficulties and purities of the human nature. In fact, poems commemorating labour bring out what was almost always in Wordsworth's mind, the communion between Man and Nature.

Storms

Wordsworth is not much concerned with violent aspects; still we find some glimpses of storms in his poetry. A reference of storm is also found in the poem "The Thorn". In fact the origin of this poem consists in a storm. Dorothy Wordsworth writes in his Journal: "W. and Basil [Montague] and I walked to the hill-tops, a very cold bleak day. We were met on our return by a severe hailstorm."[2] This is quite a familiar scene but during this storm Wordsworth's imagination was fired by a solitary aged tree. Dorothy marked the event by noting: "William wrote some lines describing a stunted thorn."[3] Later on, while describing the genesis of this poem, Wordsworth told Isaballa Fenwick:

> *"The thorn arose out of my observing on the ridge of Quantock Hill on a stormy day, a thorn which I had often passed in calm and bright weather without noticing it. I said to myself, 'Cannot I by some invention do as much to make to this thorn permanently an impressive object as the storm has made it to my eyes at this moment?'"*[4]

In his imagination, the thorn has undergone cruel experiences, exposed on the top of the mountain, it is the victim of the "stormy winter gale". "The Elegiac Stanzas" were suggested by a picture of Peele Castle in a storm by Sir Beaumont. This poem presents the contrast in view of Peele Castle in a tranquil landscape and the pictures of Peele Castle in storm. He finds no fault in picture of Beaumont. It reminds him of his brother John who had been drowned at sea. In spite of this description he has optimistic point of view as the huge castle stands sublime, braving the storm.

This sea in anger, and that dismal shore.
O 't is a passionate Work!-yet wise and well,
Well chosen is the spirit that is here;
That hulk which labours in the deadly swell,
This rueful sky, this pageantry of fear!
And this huge Castle, standing here sublime,

The picture of storm in castle inspires the individual to face the difficulties with fortitude and cheerful patience. In "Ruth" also we find a little description of storm. Ruth's lover, an American youth brings to her miseries and desolation, as his nature was made inhuman by receiving "fierce and irregular stimulus" of the tumultuous and voluptuous scenes of tropical America.

The wind, the tempest roaring high,
The tumult of a tropic sky,
Might well be dangerous food for him,
a Youth to whom was given
So much of earth – so much of heaven,
And such impetuous blood.

The poem "Resolution and Independence" opens with a storm:

There was a roaring in the wind all night;
The rain came heavily and fell in floods;

But morning is clear. Perhaps Wordsworth wants to give us a message, as the old leech gatherer is the survivor of a wife and ten children. He travels alone among the mountains and all lonely places carrying with him his fortitude and the necessities, which an unjust state of society has laid upon him. The storm is past of the leech gatherer which he had faced. This old man impresses Wordsworth.

The storm that provides modesty, dignity and charm to

Lucy proves fatal in the end. It really creates havoc as the storm comes before time and Lucy could not reach her destination. We are impressed by the sincerity and docility of the child who immediately agrees to go to town with a lantern without sparing a thought for the impending storm. The situation, however, becomes heart-rending when Lucy Gray's parents search for her all about a place in the pitch darkness of the stormy night, and then conclude that she must have died in the storm:

They wept; and turning homeward cried
'In heaven we all shall meet.

Though there is pathos in the poem, Wordsworth spiritualizes Lucy. In the whole range of Wordsworth's poetry we do not find violent aspects of nature. He searches some spiritual contentment even in storm or violent aspects of nature. The sonnet "Composed During a Storm" clearly depicts this sense:

The lingering remnant of their yellow hair,
And shivering wolves, surprised with darkness, howl
As if the sun were not. He raised his eye
Soul smitten; for, that instant did appear
Large space ('mid dreadful clouds) of perest sky,
An azure disc-shield of tranquility;
Invisible, unlooked-for, minister
Of providential goodness ever nigh!

Thus Wordsworth poetry presents an inseparable interrelation of Nature and human life in his poetry. When he thought of Nature, he thought of Man. Man is the most happy and healthy when he lives in the midst of Nature. Earth, spade and storms show his intermingling of Man and Nature.

References

1. Havens, Raymond Dexter, *The Mind of a Poet*, Baltimore, The Johns Hopkins Press, 1941, p. 74.

2. Dorothy's Journal, Quoted in *Wordsworth: A Collection of Critical Essays* (ed.), M.H. Abrams, p. 75.

3. *Ibid.*

4. *Ibid.*

10

Wordsworth's Vision of Innocence and Childhood

Innocence

Etymologically, innocence means the state of being free from sin and guilt, naïve, simplicity, ignorance etc. Romantic Poetry had a deep fascination for innocence. In contrast of eighteenth century poetry which describes fashionable society, full of artificiality and conventional style, Romantic poetry describes humbler aspects of life and simplicity. William Blake composed a number of poems entitled "Songs of Innocence". William Wordsworth, too, was down to earth simple. He is the poet of Man and not of men. He sings of the village solitaries and not of men in society. In The Preface to the 1802 edition of *The Lyrical Ballads,* he gives reasons for this preference:

> *Humble and rustic life was generally chosen, because in that condition, the essential passions of the heart find a better soil in which they can attain their maturity, are less under restraint, and seek a plainer and more emphatic language; because in that condition of life our elementary feeling co-exist in a state of greater simplicity, and consequently, may be more accurately contemplated*

and more forcibly communicated; because the manners of rural life germinate from these elementary feelings, and from the elementary character of rural occupations, they are more easily comprehended, and are more durable; and lastly, because in that condition the passions of men are incorporated with the beautiful and permanent forms of Nature.[1]

Wordsworth rediscovers the nobility and dignity of the humble and rustic life. His rustic figures are innocent, that's why they are humble. An arrogant person cannot be innocent. Wordsworth's figures may be called incarnations of innocence. Generally his adult characters suffer. In practical life, innocent people most often suffer. Just as the child is a product of Nature, Wordsworth's loveliest girls are Nature's children.

The first figure, depicting innocence, is represented by children. A study of his poems written on children can lead us to the conclusion that children attracted him by virtue of their certain peculiar, admirable qualities. One of these qualities is innocence. For example, in "We Are Seven", he tells us that he met a little girl about eight year old. He asks her how many brothers and sisters, including her, they are. She tells him that they are seven. Then she tells him that two of them lie buried in the churchyard, and yet they are seven. But he tries to correct her saying that they are five now. But she innocently replies: "Nay, we are seven."

'How many are you, then,' said I,
'If they two are in heaven?'
Quick was the little Maid's reply,
'O Master! We are seven.'
'But they are dead; those two are dead!
Their spirits are in heaven!'
'T was throwing words away; for still

The little Maid would have her will,
And said, 'Nay, we are seven!'

(We Are Seven, 61-68)

In characteristics of "A Child Three Years Old", he notices a little girl lying couched by a fern. She seems to be a favourite of Innocence:

Loving she is, and tractable, though wild;
And Innocence hath privilege in her
To dignify arch looks and laughing eyes.

Alice Fell is also an innocent child. She is too poor. Her tattered cloak gets entangled between the nave and the spokes of the poet's chaise, as she sits on the foot-hold behind the chaise. She weeps bitterly for the loss of her cloak. The poet gives her some money to buy a new cloak. The innocent child is happy like anything. Lucy, the highland girl, the Solitary Reaper and other young girls, being nature's children are innocent. Lucy Gray was the sweetest thing that ever grew /beside a human door. *"The child simply but with devastating effect completely turns the tables on the rigid world of adult experience: her innocence asserts the value of a different order of reality."*[2]

Wordsworth's second figure, obviously innocent, is young girls, though he describes them to a limited extent in early and late poetry. In some poems, like "Juvenile", the "Anacreon and Beauty" and "Moonlight", the poet describes the innocent girl in the person of his beloved. The connection between the young girl and the landscape persisted so that Wordsworth's innocent girls are nature's children. The innocence of Lucy, the Highland girl and the Solitary Reaper are beyond description. Lucy Gray, the solitary child belongs to the lonesome wild, while the Highland girl belongs to the lake, the bay, the waterfall. The poem, "She was a Phantom of Delight", describes Mary Wordsworth. Here the spirit of nature has become a woman.

A creature not too bright or good
For human nature's daily food;

"The Three Cottage Girl", written as one of the memorials of the tour on the continent in 1820, is a kind of tribute to the Highland girl. Though the poet gives each girl a local habitation—one Italian, one Helvetian, one Highland, they are images of the flowering of life.

Like child and young girl, the joyous irresponsible—who is perhaps less a recurrent figure than a convenient grouping, likewise seems an example of Wordsworth's mighty affirmation of innocence. These figures take pleasure in life and thus manifest Wordsworth's manifestation of the joy of living. The "Idiot Boy" is an example of this innocence. What wells up through the poem is the idiot boy's delight in his nocturnal excursion. When the pony moved, the boy was so delighted that he could not hold the bridle and "quite forgot his holly whip".

The fourth figure, the women are also an example of innocence and due to their innocence they become the prey of undeserved suffering. Ruth and Emily Norton are innocent sufferers. Ruth's trouble is deep rooted, having its origin in her neglected childhood. In her childhood, she had run free over hill and dale. When the gay, handsome youth from Georgia deserts her after their marriage, she goes mad. She escapes from her prison and returns to her fields. Her regression to childhood mitigates her sufferings. Emily, after the death of father and brothers is subjected to a holy "Though stern and rigorous, melancholy!" Her gloom is lightened, when the white doe has reappeared to share Emily's solitude.

The Female Vagrant, Margaret, Ruth and Emily Norton

are all essentially innocent figures. The figures of woman and child follow much the same development from unrelieved suffering to suffering tempered by religion.

Innocence appears in Wordsworth's other figures also such as the old man who first appears in the Juvenilia, No. XV, Fragment of a "Gothic" tale, presumably written about 1791. He figures the Baron Herbert of *The Borderers*. Herbert, in addition to being blind, is in exile from his rightful estate. Marmaduke in his remorse describes Herbert:

And such a man—so meek and unoffending—
Helpless and harmless as a babe; a Man
By obvious signal to the world's protection
Solemnly dedicated. (V, 2163-66)

The helplessness of man appears even more clearly in the figure of the blind beggar in *The Prelude.* Once in a London crowd Wordsworth watched the faces of the passers-by with a sense of the mystery of other lives. Far travelled in this mood, suddenly he saw the blind beggar,

Who with upright face,
Stood, propped against a wall, upon his chest.

Childhood

Wordsworth had his own way of looking at childhood. He had a high conception of childhood. His view of the child is apparent in his most popular line "the child is the father of man". The Child life is the hiding place of man's power where man must seek it within his mature faculty. The root of this feeling was Wordsworth's memory of his own childhood, so ordinary in its incidents, so marvelous in its emotions. Wordsworth's love of the child is particularly seen in these poems: "We are Seven", "There was a Boy", "The Idiot Boy", "The Immortality Ode", "The Prelude", "Lucy Gray", "The

Cuckoo" and "Alice Fell". It was not Wordsworth alone who idealized childhood. The mystics and philosophers in all ages have ever made childhood recollections the basis of their philosophical questionings. Wordsworth also speaks of his childhood recollections with a sense of gratitude:

"But for those first affections
Those shadowy recollections;
Which, be they what they may.
Are yet the fountains light of all our day,
Are yet a master light of all our seeing,

(The Immortality Ode, 149-153)

When Wordsworth returned from France as a disillusioned person, the recollections of his childhood worked as a healing balm to his wounded soul. In *The Prelude*, Book I, he recollects his childhood and says:

. . . Even then I felt
Gleams like the flashing of a shield; the earth
A common face of Nature spoke to me
Rememberable things....

(*The Prelude* I, 585-88)

Wordsworth sings in one of his inspired moments "child is the father of man". Through the recollections and observations of early childhood we may hope to trace our ancestry in heaven above or the earth beneath. In its most significant manifestations of the philosopher who wants to prove that knowledge, studies the mind of the child to show that our instinctive recognition of certain truth depends upon having been actually familiar with them in an earlier life. The Christian mystic glorifies the child for it is a state which knows no sin. Wordsworth glorifies the child but for different reasons. In many ways, he was an exceptional individual and his childhood had also been exceptional. His memories were more vivid and his thinking more penetrating than those of ordinary mortals. He finds cause for gratitude and praise in the experience of his childhood not from admiration for the child's faith in happiness, hope and liberty:

But for those questionings/Of sense and outward things/ Fallings from us, vanishing/Blank misgivings of a creature/ Moving about in worlds not realized.

The Prelude has a message for future generations; and that is, the influence of childhood on after life. Think back of your childhood, says Wordsworth, as an explanation of the problems of your life. This truth is not applicable to Wordsworth only; it is true for each one of us. Child shows the man as morning shows the day. Childhood is the golden period, the most impressionable period of one's life and it is then that though unperceived, man's future life is in the making a reference to childhood as a moulder of mature years and an inspirer of man in the later years of his life, is made by Wordsworth at the end of Book I of *The Prelude*:

Meanwhile, my hopes has been that I might fetch
Invigorating thoughts from former years,
Might fix the wavering balance of my mind
And haply meet reproaches, too, whose power
May spur me on, in manhood now mature,
To honourable toil.

(*The Prelude* I, 620-25)

In *The Prelude,* he analyzes his childhood conclusion that the child lives through the various stages in the developments of human conscious and civilization. Up to the end of his days, he cherished the memories of his childhood. Habitually his mind turned back to this source of delight. The most experiences are those, which carry him farthest on the backward road. He listens to the cuckoo with delight, for it reminds him of his school days and helps him, "to beget that golden time again". He hears the mountain echo giving back the notes of the cuckoo and at once thinks of the echoes and intelligence that comes to us we know not whence:

Such rebounds our inward ear
Catches sometimes from after-
Listens, ponders holds them dear
For of god-of God they are.

Poem after poem records the fascination that children had for him till he burst out in lyrical raptures in the sonnet "Composed on the beach near Calais":

Dear child! Dear girl that walked with me
If thou appear untouched by solemn thought,
Thy nature is not therefore less divine:
Thou lies in Abrahm's bosom all the year;
And worship'st at the Temple's inner shrine,
God being with thee when we know it not.

Wordsworth's philosophic attitude towards childhood is best represented in the "Immortality Ode". Here the child is a part symbol, part reality. Up to the VIth stanza, he presents the image of the actual child. The child is engrossed in playing with toys, which are a source of delight to him. Only the child can understand his amusements. Occasionally he is troubled by the loving kisses of his mother and the father also looks at the child with loving care. The concluding lines quietly state the activities of the child:

As if his whole vocation
Were endless imitation.

But this line also reminds us that the child has another and more real vocation—the spiritual one. Creation of the image of a living and playing child is so firm that Wordsworth is able to develop the child symbol in the next stanza without losing contact with reality. In the VIth stanza, the little child lives in his own world, not yet yoked by custom and traditions. He is happy in the midst of earthly things and soon will extinguish the divine spark, when he will be engrossed with worldly affairs. In VIIIth stanza, he represents the child:

Mighty prophet! Seer blest!
On whom those truths do rest,
Which we are toiling all our lives to find

(The Immortality Ode)

Wordsworth did not arrive at his glorification of childhood by an acquaintance with platonic philosophy, but by looking at nature and life with an open mind. Wordsworth believes that the child is endowed with vivid recollections of the precious life; hence his mind is not utterly devoid of the past glory.

Not in entire forgetfulness
And not in utter nakedness
But trailing clouds of glory do we come
From God, who is our home:
Heaven lies about us in our infancy!

(The Immortality Ode)

So long as the child remains in the state of innocence, it enjoys celestial visions; as it grows to be a man, these visions fade away and the grown up man is engrossed too much with the world. Hence Wordsworth considers the child as the "best philosopher".

Who yet dost keep
Thou best Philosopher, who yet dost keep
Thy heritage, thou Eye among the blind,

That, deaf and silent, read'st the eternal deep,
Haunted for ever by the eternal mind,

(The Immortality Ode)

He would consider himself blessed, "Could I but teach the hundredth part / Of what from thee I learn". These lines of the "Ode" remind us of the little cottage girl of "We are Seven" and the dear child of "It is a Beauteous Evening." The cottage child sings with complete confidence to her brother and sister who lies in the graveyard and young Caroline can play happily without solemn thought her nature innately. He says, "God being with thee, when we know it not." To quote Garrod about Wordsworth's faith in childhood, "*Upon the ordinary Grown man custom lies 'with a weight heavy as frost and deep almost as life'. In early childhood, and in childlike men, the bond is less heavy and intense.*"[3] The child becomes to Wordsworth the type of wisdom higher than that of the world. He prefers the faith of little children to the prejudices of grown-up men.

Let us now analyze three poems composed by Wordsworth which show us the "glory and the dream" of childhood. Wordsworth begins to live in the past. "To a Butterfly", "To the Cuckoo" and "The Rainbow" are poems of reminiscence that merges into the great "Ode" which follows immediately. The "Butterfly", "historian of my infancy", revives "dead time", of "pleasant, pleasant . . . days, when Dorothy and Wordsworth used to chase the insects with boundless joy. The "Cuckoo" brings back "tale of visionary hours" of school days, "that golden time"; while the "Rainbow", of time "when my life began". The insect, the bird, the sight are all symbols of past experiences that reveals the glory of childhood.

Not only children's glorious aspects but child psychology has also been depicted by Wordsworth. We see in "Alice Fell"— sob after sob as if her grief could never, never have an end for her tattered cloak. For that forlorn orphan girl the cloak was no less than a kingdom. Again "The Idiot Boy" also presents the child psychology. The idiot boy Johnny, with his incomprehensible but mysteriously meaningful dialogues presents a child's imagination. While writing about Johnny, Wordsworth feels like the boy Wordsworth, "grandeur in the beatings of the heart". Only Wordsworth could have written these lines:

The owlets hoot, the owlet's curr,
And Johny's lips they burr, burr, burr,
As on he goes beneath the moon.

(The Idiot Boy, 104-06)

S.B. Mukerji is of the opinion, *"It is the power and reality of that visionary world to Wordsworth and to Johnny that lent to the poem its unique appeal."*[4] The figure of the child does not appear significantly in his early poetry and it vanishes interest after 1807. Before 1798, there is only the little child whose father is mercilessly beating it in "Guilt and Sorrow". He is an image of undeserved suffering. The child figures appear especially in the period 1798-1807. Wordsworth's interest in the child seems threefold. Primarily there is the figure that belonged to memory, the child William, then there are three actual children whose psychology interested Wordsworth and most important there is the life of the spirit for which the child is a supreme symbol.

The passages in *The Prelude,* which refer most directly to childhood as such, refer to the child's creative mind. He throws light on the child's or William's early love of reading and its strengthening of imaginative life. According to Wordsworth, childhood is the great natural fact which demonstrates the perfect working of those first-born affinities that fit "Our new existence to existing things". But when Wordsworth returns to childhood in Book V, he has developed an interest that extends beyond the natural order. He says:

Our simple childhood sits upon a throne
That hath more power than all the elements
I guess not what this tells of Being past,
Nor what it argues of the life to come,
But so it is.

(The Prelude, V, 508-12)

He goes on to describe childhood as "that dubious hour, that twilight", making his meaning finally clear by calling it an

Isthmus which we cross
In progress from our native continent
To earth and human life . . .

(*The Prelude,* V, 536-38)

Here the throne of childhood seems to refer to the strength of the inner creative life. Later he remembers the spots of time in which the sense of imaginative power had been described most clearly. He writes:

Oh mystery of man, from what a depth
Proceed thy honours. I am lost but see
In simple childhood some thing of the base
On which thy greatness stands

(*The Prelude* XII, 272-75)

The child is the father of the man. Creative power depends on the ability to keep open the roads that lead each to childhood. The child is the father of the man not merely chronologically but at every instant. John Jones comments, *"Childhood is a revelation of 'our native continent', or of 'God,who is our home'; valued not for its solid and comprehensive hereness, but for its thereness, its power to illuminate the other."*[5]

Wordsworth's Childhood

Wordsworth's own childhood was not a happy one. The death of his parents, the splitting of the family, his uncomfortable relations with the grandparents, aunts and uncles at Penrith show that his life was not as happy as it appears in the poem. The opening book describes the child surrounded by love and by beneficent influences of nature. He was given full freedom and learned by experience to live wisely and well, because he was brought up by nature.

Fostered alike by beauty and by fear.

(*The Prelude* I, 302)

He enjoyed games and friendships and felt the beauty of the created world. Though he felt fear sometimes, it was a healthy and a useful fear one that convinced him that he was being watched by benevolent and corrective natural powers. To quote Fenwick notes:

In childhood . . . I was often unable to think of external things as having external existence, and I communed with all that I saw as something not apart from, but inherent in my own immaterial nature. Many times while going to school have I grasped at a wall or tree to recall myself from this abyss of idealism to the reality. At that time I was afraid of such processes.

His childhood luckily had been spent in Nature's lap. A nurse both stern and kindly, she had planted seeds of sympathy and understanding in that growing mind. He felt himself privileged, from the early days when he was to be found bathing in the stream at Cockermouth to the more mature experiences at Hawkstead. His image of himself is characteristically natural. He is a flower, sown in the right conditions and safely moved:

Fair seed time had my soul, and I grew up
Fostered alike by Beauty and by fear.

(*The Prelude* I, 301-2)

In the modern world, the growth of child in Wordsworthian way will be considered a mistake and a failure. But his way is far better. Modern docile and disciplined existence of childhood makes a kind of premature adulthood. Wordsworth rejoices in the fact that as a child he used to enjoy energetically and wholeheartedly and that he and his companions were:

A race of real children; not too wise,
Too learned, or too good; but wanton, fresh,
And bandied up and down by love and hate;
Not unresentful where self-justified;
Fierce, moody, patient, venturous, modest, shy;
Mad at their sports like withered leaves in winds;
Though doing wrong and suffering, and full oft
Bending beneath our life's mysterious weight
Of pain, and doubt, and fear, yet yielding not
In happiness to the happiness upon the earth.

(*The Prelude* V, 411-420)

The last line deals with the kind of happiness which only some fortunate children know, though the lines show the vision, hope, mistakes and enthusiasm of childhood and the inevitable journey away from the enchanted land. In the retrospective Book VIII, Wordsworth looks back at this period:

Beauteous the domain
Where to sense of beauty'
First my heart was opened.

(*The Prelude* VIII, 119-121)

In an extended piece of Miltonic pastiche, he says that his child place was, "tract more exquisitely far", and so on for some twenty tortured and elaborate lines, then suddenly he takes up a mode of sublime simplicity:

But lovelier far than this the paradise
Where I was reared . . .

Now it becomes clear that the pattern of *The Prelude* is that of an undivided *Paradise Lost*. The child is in paradise, which is lost, when he enters into manhood or in the turbulent world. The Youngman's experience of this world is an unhappy one—a world of struggle, thwarted ideals, confusion of mind. We have echoes of "Paradise lost" in his description of childhood. Wordsworth asserts his right to make an epic out of the life of a child and Youngman. "It was", he said, "but it was also he knew heroic. He makes this claim for the process of child development: 'O heavens, how awful is the might of souls'."

Thus, Wordsworth glorifies children because for him "they are the very image of god brought up in natural surroundings". His glorification of childhood has provoked a good deal of controversy, but we should remember that Wordsworth was a poet not a philosopher, and hence his conception of childhood is poetic and mystical rather than philosophical.

References

1. *Wordsworth's Poetical Works* (ed.), Thomas Hutchinson, Oxford University Press, 1910, pp.734-35.
2. Jones, Alun R., "The Compassionate World", *English,* Vol. XIX, Spring 1970, No. 103, p .8.

3. Garrod, H.W., *Wordsworth: Lectures and Essays*, London, Oxford University Press, 1923, p. 99.

4. Mukerji, S.B., *The Poetry of Wordsworth*, Vikas Publishing House Pvt. Ltd, New Delhi, 1976, p. 101.

5. Jones, John, *The Egotistical Sublime*, Chatto & Windus, 1954, p. 166.

11 Mysticism

Before describing mysticism in Wordsworth's poetry, let's have a view, what mysticism is. Mysticism is "an immediate, direct, intuitive knowledge of God or of ultimate reality attained through personal religious experience. Wide variations are found in both the form and the intensity of mystical experience."[1] Webster Dictionary defines mysticism as "The theory or belief that man can intuitively know God or religious truth, through the inward perception of the mind, a more immediate and direct method than that of ordinary understanding or sense perception." Thus, mysticism is a cognitive process as well as a mode of feeling. Quest of the invisible reality and its apprehension through contemplation or an introspective method leading to a realization of the utility of all existence, are the essential ingredients of this experience. All mystic claim, directly or by implication, immediate contact with the Transcendent through contemplation that ultimately brings about a state of bliss or serenity.

Wordsworth's interest in the subtle aspects of phenomenal existence has become proverbial. In his poems Wordsworth often describes the blessed and serene moods that revealed the mysteries of existence and invariably, lightened the burdens of many an unpleasant reality of life. From his childhood, he was given to visions. Even as a grown up man he found it impossible to shake off altogether the memory of the "black and huge peaks pursuing him with measured motion like a living thing". He was inevitably drawn to a mode of thing and tranquil recollection that is patently suggestive of mystic elements and predilections.

"In childhood", Wordsworth told Miss Fenwick, "... I was often unable to think of external things as having external existence, and I communed with all that I saw as something not apart from, but inherent in, my own immaterial nature. Many times while going to school have I grasped at a wall or tree to recall myself from this abyss of idealism to the reality. At that time I was afraid of such processes. In later periods of life I have deplored, as we have all reason to do, a subjugation of an opposite character, and have rejoiced over the remembrances, as is expressed in the lines, 'Obstinate questionings', & C."[2]

Wordsworth could recollect of occasions when as a mere boy he felt a living contact with some indefinable friendly, but bodiless presences in the world of fact and phenomena:

I felt the sentiment of Being spread
O'er all that moves and all that seemeth still;
O'er all that, lost beyond the reach of thought
And human knowledge, to thee human eye
Invisible, yet liveth to the heart;

(*The Prelude* II, 401-405)

He also vividly remembered how as a school-boy he used

to muse on "two consciousnesses, conscious of myself / and of some other Being" (*The Prelude* II, 32-33). Something like this happened to the Wanderer in his youth:

In such access of mind, in such high hour
Of visitation from the living god,
Thought was not; in enjoyment it expired.

(Excursion, 211-13)

Wordsworth had several experiences, which paved the way for later mystic experiences. These occasions were marked by "bliss ineffable", by exaltation, by a sense of divine and by something like a trance. Wordsworth refers to them as "the time in which the pulse of Being everywhere was felt", as "that bursting forth of sympathy. . . . When everywhere a vital pulse was felt"; he writes, "I, at this time, Saw blessings. . . . I was only then Contented, when . . . . I felt the sentiment of Being". This intense consciousness of the one life, which came to him when he was seventeen or eighteen and was renewed during the first year at Cambridge, may represent a late stage in the development that "perhaps started with the grasping at a stone wall while going to school and culminated in the entrance into London and in the dedication, both of which took place in a year (possibly two years) after the pulse of Being was first felt."[3]

Wordsworth's concern with the transcendent is further borne out by his occasional hallucinations and belief in genius loci. "The Haunted Tree" also bears testimony to his awareness of some invisible form of being. Moreover, the numerous references to soul, amplitude and the sublime in his works further suggests his preoccupation with a universe beyond the world of eye and ear. His keen and unflagging interest in solitude also seems to point in the same direction. Mystics have always aspired for and valued this peculiar kind of solitude as a prelude to spiritual enlightenment. St. Augustine prescribes loneliness and silence as ideal conditions for communion with God, while St. Teresa's visions are known to have been preceded by a feeling of awesome solitude of dereliction.

In former mysticism, the state of darkness of spiritual groping precedes the phase of illumination. Wordsworth too seemed to have passed through a similar experience before gaining his illuminating visions of reality. In *The Prelude* the account of Snowdon enshrouded in moonlight and "the silent sea of hoary mist" has a touch of numinous about it. It may be argued that these visions might have been inspired by some actual physical phenomena, but Wordsworth's known habit of poetizing the objects of nature and the apocalyptic character of the former view suggest mystical overtones rather than a realistic description of the landscape.

Contemplation as a means of attaining spiritual edification and the final beatitude forms as integral part of religious mysticism, and as such Wordsworth's interest in it is rather significant. He has repeatedly used the term "meditation". He called *The Prelude* a "meditative history". His theories of 'emotions recollected in tranquility' imply a contemplative process not very different from the contemplative stage in formal mysticism. Many passages in *The Prelude* present a yearning for and harmonizing with the inner life of nature as the mystics seek in the divine being.

Concept of universal kinship is inseperably connected with the formal mystic tradition. It has mainly been derived from Plato's theory of the phenomenal world which is a shadow of the Absolute Reality existing as an Idea in the Ineffable Mind, belief in the inherent unity of all existence had acquired special significance for Christian mystics. Plotinus who interpreted Plato's metaphysics, laid the foundations of Neo-Platonism. It was often called the nurse of Christian speculative thought. The soul's yearning for merging in the infinite, and its experience of disembodied union with the latter constitute the highest form of joy, termed by the Western mystics as "Ecstasy". "Wordsworth's mystic view of the inner relationship in a unicentric universe impelled by a common soul, and his cosmic sympathy are thus distant echoes of the Plotinian concept of an informed and living universe."[4] In moments of deeper insights he passionately realized and sang of this spiritual affinity between man and nature:

A sense sublime
Of something far more deeply interfused,
Whose dwelling is the light of setting suns,
And the round ocean and the living air,
And the blue sky, and in the mind of man:
A motion and a spirit, that impels
All thinking things, all objects of all thought,
And rolls through all things.

(Tintern Abbey, 95-102)

Again in the "Tintern Abbey" we are told about this unifying force that "from link to link—it circulates the soul of all the worlds"—the links remind one of the Plotinian chain of being. Nature mysticism is directly related to the theory of universal kinship. Early Christian fathers, like St. Cyril and St. Basil, had also recommended the contemplation of natural phenomena as an aid to the appreciation of divine glory. St. Francis of Assissi, whom Wordsworth reverently remembers in "The Cuckoo of Lavarna", is known to have contemplated before birds, flowers and insects and expressed a desire to preach to "my little sisters, the birds". Nearer home, the Cambridge Platonists also approved of the meditative study of nature of purposes. Apart from his personal predilections, there was a strong religious and literary tradition as well to give Wordsworth's instinctive love for nature a mystic pattern. To the young boy she was a 'passion', "an appetite" and a feeling and a love:

That had no need for a remoter charm
By thought supplied, nor any interest
Unborrowed from the eye.

(Tintern Abbey, 81-83)

To Wordsworth Nature was not only imbued with a merely passive, animistic existence; but also endowed with consciousness as well. She was kind, sensitive and responsive to man's interest in her. Like the Plotinian deity, she even attracted her admirers and enjoyed shedding her benevolent influence on them. She never betrayed "the heart that loved her", so the poet is prompted by this innate love. He rejoiced in being her worshipper and gratefully pledged deeper loyalty to her. The faith, thus reposed, yielded happier results; for nature did not only lighten his pensive moods, but provided food for future thoughts as well. In the hour of crisis she rescued him from utter "dereliction and dismay", and preserved the final serenity of his mood:

The gift is yours,
Ye winds and sounding cataracts!'tis yours
Ye mountains! Thine, O nature! Thou hast fed
My lofty speculations and in thee,
For this uneasy hearts of ours, I find
A never failing principle of joy
And purest passion.

(*The Prelude* II, 445-51)

Landscapes provided him refreshing memories that sustained his mind and heart in the turbulent life of London.

He found the same kind of sincerity, exclusive love, self effacement and complete identification with nature as in the meditations of devout mystics.

Wordsworth's philosophy of Nature also contains some pantheistic trends. In pantheism, the doctrine of the translation of the One into Many receives theological sanction. Wordsworth rejoiced not only in discovering a common soul running through the round ocean, the blue sky, the setting sun and the mind of a man, but he assigned to nature the superior role of a teacher, a spiritual nurse and the harbinger of mystic insights also. In brief, she was fully divinized:

Nature through all conditions hath a power
To consecrate, if we have eyes to see,
The outside of her creatures, and to breathe
Grandeur upon the very humblest face
Of human life.

(*The Prelude* XII, 282-86)

Wordsworth's concept of nature seems to resemble in some measure the Vedantic doctrine of the divine Maya. A patently mystic approach on the poet's part is undeniable. Gratitude, hopefulness and spontaneity of faith characterize the mystic view of religion.

Integral parts of Christian mysticism have three distinct stages of spiritual ascent—the purgative, the illluminative, and the unitive. In the first stage, the meditator seeks to purge himself of all temporal interests and the conventional impediments to spiritual progress. Thus purified, the seeker prepares himself for the illuminative stage of contemplation. In this stage, the clouds of "unknowing" are dispelled, and the devotee feels himself enwrapped in the light of "knowing" and love. The third stage brings about complete spiritual union with the Ineffable, culminating in the attendant experience of rapturous joy—the Ecstasy. A closer study of Wordsworth's poetry of nature, specially his attitude to nature, seems to suggest a fairly correspondent pattern. Though, he had an instinctive love for nature since childhood, his kinship with nature reaffirmed in mature days. Wordsworth recalled how in moments of spiritual perplexity, he warred against himself and

Like a cowed monk who hath forsworn the world,
Zealously laboured to cut off my heart
From all the sources of her former strength.

(*The Prelude* XII, 78-80)

In order to express his desire for solitude and isolation, the poet has aptly used the monk simile. His progressive concentration on nature and withdrawal from material pursuits led to the love of man and even divulged

Those mysteries of being which have made
And shall continue evermore to make
Of the whole human race one brotherhood.

(*The Prelude* XII, 85-87)

Corresponding to these formal stages in the mystic ascent are the successive experiences of fear, love and joy. Of these, fear, apart from its psychological validity, seems to have Biblical affirmation too. The awesome majesty of nature exercised simultaneously the antithetical influences of fear and fascination, which largely determined his future spiritual attitudes:

Fair seed time had my soul, and I grew up
Fostered alike by beauty and fear.

(*The Prelude* I, 301-02)

Sublimation of fear engenders love that is an unerring

guide to higher spiritual knowledge. Wordsworth acknowledged an abiding debt, "to fear and love, to love as prime and chief, for the far ends" (*The Prelude* XIV, 160-162).

Love dispelled the fear of the invisible and charged the dreadful sights and sounds of nature with deeper meaning and significance. Without love man could not even qualify for his great spiritual heritage, nor was he capable of retaining the magnificence of his status without it. Love is the natural and inviolable bond between God and man. Love of nature leads to love of man, and this all-embracing affection is the source of genuine piety, faith and lasting spiritual delight.

Meditative devotees eagerly cherish and long for ecstasy and ultimate joy which results from mystical union with the Absolute. Wordsworth's poems abound in impassioned utterances that are admittedly mystical in their intensity and effect. To his joy was the highest gift of nature. Wordsworth is unable to relate what happened during these moments of ecstatic emancipation. Like all mystics, he exclaims:

Alas! I feel
That I am trifling: 'twas a moment's pause.
All that took place within me, came and went
As in a moment, and I only now
Remember that it was a thing divine.

(*The Prelude* VIII, A705-09)

He enjoyed a kind of spontaneous, "religious love" for nature that endowed him with visions of glory. Under this influence, even the grim and terror-striking aspects were transmuted and deepened the poet's sense of gratitude and joy. Here the most noteworthy thing is that the formal mystic hoards his experience of joy, Wordsworth rejoiced in transmitting it to others as well. His mysticism was not a passive, self-enclosed, cloistral mysticism; it was genuinely poetic. Common psychic experiences of religious mystics are voices and visions. Prophets are known to have heard divine voices in secluded caves and mountains. We can quote the examples of St. John's Apocalypse, the visions of Suso, St. Teresa, Jacob, Boehme, Blake and Yeats. Wordsworth also mentions the "audible seclusions" of "bare hills and valleys, full of caverns, rocks" (*The Prelude* VIII, 634) and the repeated references to the sounding cataracts and trumpeting winds.

The three types of mystic visions are intellectual, imaginary and corporeal. The intellectual vision is a spontaneous, bodiless and nonsensorial revelation, not easily describable in words, and yet real and vividly realized. In it a mystic is aware of some invisible being and latent beauty. The poet's vision of intellectual vision may be seen in the soul rising like a star elsewhere and trailing clouds of glory from God, and its darkening progress in the material world. The following lines may be cited as an illustration of the same:

To unorganic natures were transformed
My own enjoyments: or the power of truth
Coming in revelation, did converse
With things that really are; I, at this time,
Saw blessing spread around me like a sea.

(*The Prelude* II, 391-95)

It is difficult to distinguish between intellectual and imaginary visions; for both are non-sensorial in essence and proceed from the mystics' passion for spiritual reality. The pictures of countless daffodils flashing upon the inward eye or Wordsworth's vision of the ethereal unsubstantial world evoked by the cuckoo's songs come in this category. A vision conjured by the landscape enveloped in mist and moonlight present this effect:

Gently did my soul
Put off her veil, and self-transmuted, stood
Naked as in the presence of God.

The corporeal or physical visions of mystics are presented in Solitary's apocalyptic vision of the city of glory and the "revealed abode" of beatified spirits. Peculiar physical manifestations and reactions, such as benumbing of senses of bodily movements and respiration also characterize genuine mystic trances. St. Teresa has given an account of mental and physical states resulting from her spiritual visions. Wordsworth's version of his own "serene and blessed moods" also contains features of physical insensibility, pulselessnes and the cessation of breath before spiritual illumination and final communion:

The affections lead us on,
Until, the breath of this corporeal frame
And even the motion of our human blood
Almost suspended, we are laid asleep
In body, and become a living soul:
While with an eye made quiet by the power
Of harmony, and the deep power of joy,
We see into the life of things.

(Tintern Abbey, 42-49)

Psychologically speaking, mysticism may be classified into two types—extrovertive and introvertive. The extrovertive is concerned with the Beyond, the Absolute reality both transcendental and immanent. In Christian history, the antinomian sects and the thirteenth-century order of the Brethern of Free Spirit represent this type in its extreme form. This attitude often encourages the growth of apparently pantheistic tendencies as it is allied to the Platonic doctrine of Reality. It is this kind of mystic experience that has usually inspired poetic mysticism such as we find in the works of Vaughan, Traherne and Wordsworth. The introvertive type is more subjective in nature and therefore richer in the quality of inwardness. In devotional contexts the introvertive trend has generally found expression in two opposite directions—the enlargement and projection of the self by way of its absorption in the complete oblivion of all external phenomena, to a state of experience that may be described in Donne's phrase, used in a different context, as "Nothing Else is". While the extrovertive leads to inner harmony and joy through knowledge of things. Wordsworth's mysticism belongs to this total non-duality of existence was not always within his reach. In moments of inspiration he seems to span the gulf between the visible and the invisible, the transitory and the eternal, the ethereal and the substantial; but his mysticism remains earth-bound in its ultimate effect, irradiating the life of sense and reason and fortifying the poet with knowledge, will and power to edify mankind at large:

Prophets of nature, we to them will speak
A lasting inspiration, sanctified
By reason, blest by faith: what we have loved,
Others will love, and we will teach them how;
Instruct them how the mind of man becomes
A thousand times more beautiful than the earth
On which he dwells . . .

(*The Prelude* XIV, 444-50)

Reason shares the laurels with faith now, which is rather significant. Inspiration and faith, the twin ingredients of mysticism, still hold their ground, and their validity is assessed and confirmed by reason. This triple alliance explains the uneven quality of Wordsworth's poetry. It also accounts for the frequency and peculiar character of his visions that often approximate to the ecstatic moods of religious mystics.

Thus unquestionably, Wordsworth's mystical experiences had much to do with the distrust of the intellect and with the intense consciousness of the mysteries of being. They must have strengthened his faith in the reality of the unseen and deepened the conviction that the spiritual life is nourished chiefly through communion with nature. Undoubtedly, Wordsworth derived the inspiration, the vision, and the dynamics of his life from these moments of transcendent ecstasy.

References

1. Funk and Wagnalls, *New Encyclopaedia,* Vol. 18, p. 228.
2. Fenwick note to the Immortality Ode, quoted from Reymond Dexter Haven, *The Mind of a Poet* , Baltimore, The Johns Hopkins Press, 1941, pp. 155-56.
3. Raymond and Dexter Havens, *The Mind of a Poet*, p. 171.
4. Hasan, Masoodul, "Mystical Elements in Wordsworth's Poetry", *Essays on Wordsworth: A Bi-Centenary Tribute* (ed.), Asloof Ahmed Ansari, Department of English, A.M.U., Aligarh, 1973, p. 85.

12

Moral Tone

The love of Nature is to be found in all the English poets, from Chaucer downward. In Wordsworth's own day, many other poets were writing poems thoroughly impregnated with the love of Nature, but Wordsworth's treatment of Nature is different from others. He unfolded a new and individual view of Nature. He differs from all other poets in the stress he puts upon the moral influences of Nature. "He loves her as he might love a mistress, and communes with her as mind may commune with mind. To him she is a vast embodied Thought, a presence not merely capable of inspiring delightful ardour, but of elevating man by noble discipline."[1]

In common things that round us lie
Some ransom truths he can impart.

When we think about the moral characteristics of Wordsworth's poetry, we find that it excites in us many emotions, but they are always pure and ennobling emotions. Rev. F.W.Robertson says,

> *In reading Wordsworth the sensation is as the sensation of the pure water drinker, whose palate is so refined that he can distinguish between rill and rill, river and river, fountain and fountain, as compared with the obtuse sensations of him who has destroyed the delicacy of his palate by grosser libations, and who can distinguish no difference between water and water, because to him all pure things are equally insipid.*[2]

There is a gravity and sweetness in Wordsworth's poems, which could only spring from a noble nature, dedicated to the daily contemplation of lofty purposes. Man can rise above his suffering by calling to his aid his own moral strength. He feels remoteness from all sordid aims and debasing passions, and he calls us to a higher, a simpler and a serene life.

> *He preaches to an age corrupted with sensationalism the joy that lies in natural emotions; to an age stung with the hunger for impossible ideals the attainable valour and nobility of homely life; ... to the worldly he speaks of unworldliness; to the perplexed, of trust; to the victims of vain perturbation and disquiet, of peace.*[3]

Wordsworth's description of green solitudes of lake and mountain presents an ineffable and almost saintly charm. He breathes consolation and encouragement into tired hearts and failing spirits. He is the apostle of peace, the minister of cleansing to his time. He may have nothing new or startling to say. He sings of love and duty, of disciplined desires and purged and regulated passions, but his voice is that of a great prophet, who speaks words, which are for the healing of the nations. He rouses us from languor, because, in spite of his calmness there is mixed a strenuous and eager spirit, conscious of a Divine mission, and bent on its fulfillment. It is this moral pre-eminence of Wordsworth, which is the secret of his mastery over such very different minds as Mill's and Ruskin's, George Eliot's, and Arnold's. It is largely his moral fervour, which has given him priesthood in literature and surrounded his memory with a sort of secret halo.

Wordsworth once wrote to his friend Sir George Beaumont, "Every great poet is a great teacher; I wish to be considered as a teacher or as nothing." In his view every great poet is a prophet and seer, and therefore, also a teacher. Thus, he combines, as every poet does, the function of a poet and a teacher. How does a poet teach? He teaches not by giving out moral precepts and maxims, as a moralist or theologian does; he teaches by presenting before the world a new vision of life. This new vision that the poet discloses is not only beautiful and glorious, but also provides to us a new angle from which to look at life. In one of his letters to Lady Beaumont the poet observed:

> *There is scarcely one of my poems which do not aim to direct the attention to some moral sentiment or to some general principle or law of thought, or of our intellectual constitution. ... my writings (and among them these little Poems) will cooperate with the benign tendencies in human nature and society, wherever found; and that they will, in their degree, be efficacious in making men wiser, better and happier.*[4]

On another occasion, he explained his aim in writing poetry to Lady Beaumont:

> *To console the afflicted, to add sunshine to day-light by making the happy happier, to teach to the young and the gracious of every age, to see, to think, and to feel, and, therefore, to become more actively and securely virtuous.*[5]

Accordingly, critics have found the poetry of Wordsworth "as a great nourisher and stimulant", and as "the very culture of feeling and as moral and didactic". Wordsworth had a tendency to generalize his experiences and to draw moral lessons from them so as to ensure that the reader did not miss a point. Wordsworth wanted to cooperate his poetry with "the benign tendencies in human nature in making man nobler, purer and better". A study of his poetry enables his readers to think on man, nature and human life and thus answers the question of moral tone in his poetry. His message to humanity and his teachings are basically moral in tone.

Wordsworth's morals were not simple one as he had a great love for humanity. In *The Prelude* (X, 266-272; XI 173-178) Wordsworth gives us a glimpse into the convulsions of his soul. His moral nature suffered a lot with the England's declaration of war against the liberties of France. Let us pause to grasp fully Wordsworth's predicament at this stage—the grave crisis he was passing through: on the one hand, in personal life, remorse for Annette Vallon episode and dark uncertainty about his own future; on the other, the props he had built his golden dream on—faith in man, in France, in the Revolution, in the regeneration of mankind—all crumbling down one after another. The Prelude vivifies the predicament:

> *. . . So I fared,*
> *dragging all precepts, judgments, maxims, creeds,*
> *Like culprits to the bar;*
> *. . . now believing,*
> *Now disbelieving; endlessly perplexed*
> ....
> *Sick, wearied out with contraries,*
> *Yielded up moral questions in despair.*

(*The Prelude* XI, 293-305)

The word "moral" is the key to the understanding of this passage, since the problems which troubled Wordsworth were no longer those of politics but of morality. The first teaching of Wordsworth is that man should approach Nature in the right mood, which is defined as a mood of "wise passiveness" with a "heart that watches and receives". Wisdom, truth, joy and peace are qualities that exist outside of man and may pass into his life from Nature, if he approaches it in a mood of "wise passiveness". This moral tone in Wordsworth's poetry is most apparent in his nature poetry. From Nature man can get moral lesson:

One impulse from a vernal wood
May teach you more of man,
Of moral evil and of good,
Than all the sages can.

(The Tables Turned)

It was Wordsworth's faith that Nature teaches wisdom, truth and reality of things. One moment of communion with Nature may give us more of wisdom than many years of reason can give:

One moment now give us more
Than fifty years of reason.

Much the same thing may be said of the poet's more deliberate assertion that he was:

Well pleased to recognize
In nature and the language of the sense
The anchor of my purest thoughts, the nurse,
The guide, the guardian of my heart, and soul
Of all my moral being.

(Tintern Abbey, 107-11)

To be sure, his inheritance and early training, his growing up in an atmosphere of real piety, affection and liberty, his association with men, women and boys of character was the backbone of his moral being. This he overlooks; yet without it the forests and streams might have had no effect upon him morally or might have moved him as the landscape of Georgia did Ruth's lover. As the sun is called the life of the world although it can do nothing without earth and moisture, so Wordsworth termed nature the soul of his moral being because it was the dynamic force in his ethical life. What was vital and fundamental in his morality and attitude towards life came to him not from books' precepts or institutions, but through the senses from the ever-living universe. Wordsworth speaks of Nature's lore:

Sweet is the lore which Nature brings;
Our meddling intellect
Mis-shapes the beauteous forms of things
We murder to dissect.

According to Wordsworth, reason is discursive; it is powerless to attain truth. Nature manifests itself as a beautiful unity. Reason fails to grasp this unity.

False secondary power
By which we multiply distinctions; then,
Deem that our puny boundaries are things
That we perceive, and not that we have made.

Wordsworth gives the message of a moral and virtuous life in his poetry. In "The Character of the Happy Warrior", he explains the mode in which a grand character can be formed.

He deals in his poetry not with the lives and doings of the kings and his generals, the great and the rich, but with those of the humble shepherds, farmers, leach-gatherers, etc., of Cumberland. Though they are poor and suffering, they are contented. These simple characters are held out as examples to show that true happiness is to be sought not in external conditions, but in the soul. It may be had even without money and without price, through a life of faith, fortitude, virtue and self sacrifice. Wordsworth found a justification for dwelling on rural life because in such life passions are associated with the beautiful and permanent forms of nature. The sensations received by man in natural surroundings become the source not only of joy but morality also. The peasant heroes of Wordsworth were all inspired by higher and nobler ideals of life and they proved to be beacon lights of hope for erring humanity. As man has no innate ideas, so also he has no innate morality. Man's moral sense develops by associating pleasurable sensations with certain objects. By associating himself with objects which are not harmful, man perfects his moral nature. Here Rousseau helped Wordsworth.

The poem "Resolution and Independence" is in fact a sort of moral lesson both to the poet himself and the readers. The old leech-gatherer has been presented more as a prophet, a seer and a diviner than as an ordinary old man. The life of the old man carries on his business of leech-gathering, even though "they have dwindled long by slow decay". He still "persevere and find them where I may". He reveals to the poet's conscience some vital truths of life and dragged him out of the morass of pessimism and despair in which he had been engulfed; therefore, Wordsworth finally reaches a conclusion:

"God", said I, "be my help and stay secure
I'll think of the leech-gatherer on the lonely moor".

Thus the old leech-gatherer teaches courage, fortitude, perseverance, and above all, resolution and independence. The poem "Goody Blake and Harry Gill" also presents moral tone. The poem is a moral tale of a well-to-do farmer and a poor old woman. Goody Blake is a representative of oppressed, cold and desperate humanity while Harry is a representative of the acquisitive and possessive property ownership denounced by Rousseau. The ballad, said Crabb Robinson, showed qualities that were "Truly Shakespearean". In its repetition of simple phrases and dwelling on simple incidents merely by recording the story, the narrator is indicating his moral position, especially when he alters the original narrative in Goody Blake's favour.

Wordsworth's moral vein is seen in a number of poems. His strong moral and philosophical convictions which he professed to teach are embodied in poems like "Intimations of Immortality" and "Ode to Duty". "In Intimations of Immortality", the poet works upon the conviction: "Child is the Father of man." Child, who comes with clouds of heavenly glory gradually, forgets his pre-natal experiences as it grows up. The grown-up man can realize by recalling his childhood experiences, that the soul is immortal. The whole poem is reflective and meditative, teaching such profound ideas about Nature as the following:

To me the meanest flower that blows can give
Thoughts that do often lie too deep for tears.

Apparently, the poem carries a certain ethical purpose where the poet talks about the soothing thoughts that spring out of human sufferings. Wordsworth believed that following the path of Duty and Morality one could rise to noble heights of success in his life. It was not the life of debauchery and licentiousness that could bring man to real happiness in his life. Real happiness in life comes by leading a life of morality, duty and simplicity these facts are emphasized by Wordsworth in "Michael" and "Ode to Duty". In "Michael" Wordsworth admonishes the readers not to follow the evil ways of Luke who had belied all hopes and expectations of poor Michael and brought despair in life. "Ode to Duty" is a landmark in the history of the poet's mind. It is a unique combination of sublimity of thought, grandeur of morality and excellence of poetry. His "Ode to Duty" is a message about the importance of duty in life. The secret of real happiness, both within and without, lies in the performance of one's duty. Duty is a source of wisdom, humility and spirit of self-sacrifice. "Ode to Duty" is the poetic embodiment of the ideal which he pursued in his own life and which he showed up before the world. Wordsworth calls Duty a stern law-giver—the "stern daughter of the voice of God". If we obey her command,

Serene will be our days and bright,
And happy will our nature be,
When love is an erring light,
And joy its own security.
And they a blissful course may hold
Even now, who, not unwisely bold,
Live in the spirit of this creed;
Yet seek thy firm support, according to their need.

Even Nature works according to the dictates of duty:

Flowers laugh before thee on their beds;
And fragrance in thy footing treads;
Thou dost preserve the stars from wrong;
And the most ancient heavens, through Thee
are fresh are strong.

Wordsworth's most significant message to humanity is the message of "plain living and high thinking". He wishes his readers to become:

Type of the wise who soar, but never roam;
True to the kindred point of Heaven and Home!

(To a Skylark)

The poet warns his countrymen of the evils of worldliness and gross materialism. He wanted human beings to keep away from the life of sordid materialism for such a life was neither useful to the individual nor good for the society which pursued it. He expresses his resentment in the following lines of the sonnet:

> *The world is too much with us; late and soon,*
> *Getting and spending, we lay waste our powers,*
> *Little we see in Nature that is ours.*

He believes that even a superstitious veneration of the forces of Nature is better than apathy born of absorption in materialistic things. In his classical poem "Laodameia", he concentrated not on the tumult and turbulence of passion but on the control that a good wife ought to exercise on her emotional exuberance. The message in "Laodameia":

> *Control rebellious passions, for the God's approve,*
> *The depth and not the tumult of the soul.*

Wordsworth believed that human life was worth living in spite of the sorrows and the sufferings that may come to assail it from time to time. Suffering was, in fact, a means to an ethical end. "The still sad music of humanity" is neither harsh nor grating and has ample power to chasten and subdue. Man can lift above the suffering by calling to his help the strength of his moral life and the resources of divine Providence.

Wordsworth's poems have great moral value. As Legouis says, "the *Lyrical Ballads* and the poems of the same group are a series of moral analysis of a rich intrinsic value, discreetly guided by edifying and utilitarian purpose".[6] To many of readers Wordsworth has given a glimpse of "truths that wake to perish never"; while even to those for whom his mysticism carries no inspiration there are touches like this, splendid in its stoical fortitude.

> *We men that in our morn of youth defied*
> *The elements, must vanish; be it so!*

Thus, Wordsworth knows the conflict in which human nature is involved. He as a priest of Nature exhorts us to learn from Nature. He is familiar with the prime values for continuing existence and growth. He is the poet of moral strenuousness and tension of the fortitude and patience. This moral pre-eminence is the secret of Wordsworth's mastery over such different persons as Mill, Ruskin, George Eliot and Arnold. It is largely also his moral fervour which has given him a species of priesthood in literature and surrounded his memory with a sort of sacred halo.

References

1. Dawson, W.J., *The Makers of Modern English*, Shalabh Book House, Meerut, p. 118.
2. *Ibid.*, p. 112.
3. *Ibid.*, p. 113.
4. *The Letters of William and Dorothy Wordsworth*, Vol. I (ed.), Ernest De Selincourt, Oxford 1937-39, quoted in Herbert Read, *Wordsworth*, pp. 161-62.
5. *Ibid.*, p. 161.
6. Legouis and Cazamian, *History of English Literature*, Macmillan India Limited, p. 1005.

13
Diction

God wove a web of loveliness
Of clouds and stars and birds
But made not anything at all
So beautiful as word

—Anna H. Branch

Diction is the vehicle of thoughts and words are the clothes that thoughts wear. Beautiful words are indeed and in fact the very light of the spirit. Words are of paramount importance in the study of literary composition. Diction usually seeks to observe two principal criteria: fitness to theme, mood, and purpose and to sustain interest variety. The problem is to determine which words fit. Advantages of using the common terms have well been pointed out by Joubert, "It's through familiar words that the style bites into the reader. It's through them that great thoughts gain currency and are taken in good faith. . . ."[1]

There is a difference between the diction of poetry and the diction of prose. Here, we are concerned with poetry only.

Poetry not only speaks to the intellect, but is directed to the emotions as well. "In the style of poetry", says Joubert, "each word reverberates like the note of well-tuned lyre, and always leaves behind it a multitude of vibrations."[2] Suggestions, the connotation of words constitute in large degree the very stuff with which the poet works. Poetry is the successful blending of the undefined and the defined in words that constitutes the triumph of the poet's art.

In English poetry, diction has always associated itself with the natural speech of the time. Wordsworth did not like the trend of poetic diction prevalent before him. He called it "vicious poetic diction". In 1798, he turned the whole tradition of English poetry and emancipated it from the tyranny of wit-writing, which had lasted for about a century and a half. All his efforts were concentrated on this end—the return of naturalism and simplicity of diction. He declares that "there neither is, nor can be any essential difference between the language of prose and metrical composition" and he intends to adopt and imitate "the very language of men". He was partly right. If these statements were taken as general rules, they would outlaw most of the poetry before Wordsworth's time and much of his own; they should be understood in their place, as prefatory explanation of his particular purpose in writing *Lyrical Ballads.* Nevertheless Wordsworth determined the course of poetry in the nineteenth century. Shelley, Keats, Landor, Tennyson and Swinburne were all affected by the revolution in poetic diction initiated by Wordsworth.

Wordsworth was not only a poetic thinker but also a literary artist. He adopted various literary forms—the narrative, the lyrical, the elegiac and the sonnet. He studied sonnet. He studied the organization and interpretation of reflective poems of the 18th century. His heroic poetry is sometimes cast into heroic metre, sometimes into that of the ballad but in each medium he achieved distinction. His earliest poems "An Evening Walk" and "Descriptive Sketches" are written in Miltonic or Spenserian stanzas.

In 1798, Wordsworth, in collaboration with Coleridge published a poem collection entitled *Lyrical Ballads with a Few Other Poems*. It shows that certain poems are different from others, that is, not of that kind. Some poems are in ballad form written in narrative to be sung and some are in lyric form, simple subjective and non-narrative songs. "Goody Blake and Harry Gill", "The Thorn", and "The Idiot Boy" are the only real ballads by Wordsworth in the volume. There are, however, several other poems which approximate to ballads, such as "The Female Vagrant", "We are Seven", "Simon Lee", and "The Last of the Flock" or at least, are narrative or anecdotal poems. There are also a number of poems, such as "The Mad Mother" and "The Complaint of a Forsaken Indian Woman" that are really songs and some pieces such as "The Tables Turned" and "Lines Written in Early Spring" which may be lyrical but hardly deserve to be called ballads. This volume is unified, of course, not by any prevailing type of poetry represented, in spite of the expectations aroused by the title, but by the uniformity of poetic style. Ballads were commonly written in those days but Wordsworth and Coleridge had the folk ballads prominently in mind and followed the commonest ballad stanza of the 15th century, a quatrain with four beats in the first and third lines and three beats in second and fourth lines. In the folk ballads, the first and third lines were unrhymed, probably because the stanzas were septenary couplets, broken by a pause after the eighth syllable. The ballad stanza differs from the common measure of hymns only-but for Wordsworth notably—by its metrical irregularity. Kinship of ballad and hymns appears most strikingly in the diminished second and fourth lines.

Wordsworth was "among the earliest practicing poets to follow the theory of the accentual base rather than the theory of syllable counting in English verse". "Tintern Abbey" is an indisputable example. Wordsworth tried in *Lyrical Ballads* to suggest the naivette of folk ballads through rhythms. The deliberately low simplicity of the language makes the accentuation of these verses generally indistinguishable from syllable counting. His ballad verse may have not the fire and lilt of Scott, but they exhibit often a simple force and chaste tenderness unmatched by his contemporaries.

Wordsworth experiments with various mixtures of method in Lyrical Ballads as "The Mad Mother" and "The Complaint of the Forsaken Indian Woman" are first person monologues, though not in any Browning sense dramatic. "Goody Blake and Harry Gill", "The Last of the Flock" and "Anecdote for Fathers" approximate to straight narrative with neutral narrator. Whatever may be the experiments, Wordsworth discovered an almost uniform excellence of dialogue in traditional ballads. After simplicity of diction, the most pervasive device in his short poems is dialogue. Dialogue is central in "We are Seven", "The Fountain", "The Idiot Boy", "Expostulation and Reply" and even "Michael".

"Simon Lee" begins as a narrative poem. Its gait and its language are clumsy, even ludicrous. The first eight stanzas present a kind of narrative. Then Wordsworth changes the point of view. He breaks into the story and addresses the reader directly. He does this by stopping the narrative and stepping into the poem in a most unobtrusive way, though perhaps disingenuous manner. After sixty nine lines Wordsworth proceeds to dramatize the incident of "Simon Lee". The method of "Simon Lee" is characteristic of the poetic procedure adopted by Wordsworth in the 1798 *Lyrical Ballads* as a whole.

The poem, "We are Seven" presents a dialogue between an adult and a little cottage girl, who is eight year old. The form is fitted to content. Both the questioner and the child speak a plain diction devised and conventionalized by Wordsworth. From the simplicity of diction, we have the satisfying illusion that the adult stoops to the vocabulary of the eight year old. Wordsworth has modified the ballad stanza in this poem, by rhyming the first and the third lines except in the concluding stanza, where an extra line is added after the third to form a rhyming couplet.

But they are dead; those two are dead
Their spirits are in heaven!
'twas throwing words away; for still
The little maid would have her will,
And said, 'Nay, we are seven!

This poem is closed to the hymnal common measure than to ballads, as the iambic beat of this poem is deliberately monotonous with few variations. Four poems of simple diction in *Lyrical Ballads* are openly didactic. They illustrate Wordsworth's ideas and beliefs. These poems are "Lines Written in Early Spring", "To my Sister", "Expostulation and Reply" and "Tables Turned". The language of these poems does not suggest the naiveté of either peasant or child. It is the language of a poet disciplined to simplicity. "The Tables Turned" modifies the ballad stanza only by cross rhyming a4- b3- a4- b3, the other three extend the second line to four feet, a4-b4, a4,b3. They seem less discursive but offer cryptic earnest declaration. By their succinctness, plain talk and cool judgement, they achieve wit in a dignified sense. None of the four doctrinal poems contains striking metaphors. All contain aphorisms: "We murder to dissect", "One moment now may give us more, than years of toiling reason". They contain bare precept, "come forth and feel the sun". The shortened line of each stanza makes possible a concentration of gnomic power. Except "The Tables Turned" the final line of each poem is a repetition. The rule of simplicity relaxes enough for lines of subtle metrics to follow or usher in a string of monosyllables. Their most obvious device in conveying the theme is memorable exaggeration:

One impulse from a vernal wood
May teach you more of man
of moral evil and of good,
Than all the sages can.

The memorableness comes partly from the pattern of sounds: the rhymes (*man, than, can*); the alliteration *(one, wood, may, more, man, moral*); consonance (*more, moral);* repetition of vowels; and the more complex patterns *(from a vernal, more of, of moral evil,* where the sounds of *vernal* echo as far away as *evil,* and the order of consonants, *frmvrnl, nrf, fmrlvl,* tells why). These patterns resound much more insistently than similar patterns in the blank verse of "Tintern Abbey" and *The Prelude,* not only because of the shorter, rhyming lines, but also because of the iambic regularity of gnomic poems. Before the second and third editions of *Lyrical Ballads* in 1800 & 1802, Wordsworth practiced new refinements in his technique of lyric simplicity; it can be seen in "A Poet's Epitaph", "To Sexton", "Lucy Poems" and "Matthew Poems".

Among the most famous five elegiac pieces known as Lucy Poems, four are in the ballad stanza modified by cross-rhyming, a4-b3-a4-b3. The exception, "Three Years She Grew in Sun and Shower," extends the stanza to six lines by the creation of couplets: a4-a4-b3-c4-c4-b3. Wordsworth varied the order of the poems, and he did not ever print them together as a group. Lucy and Matthew pieces are more intricate than the gnomic poems of 1798. They counter pose spondees, trochees and occassionally anapests upon the iambic base.

"The Thorn", a great and remarkable poem, is extremely simple in language, suiting the simplicity of the theme. It is free from any touch of the poetic, artificial or grandiose. In this poem, there is not one word that is hard to understand, and the only figure of speech is a simile comparing one ordinary object to another:

There is a thorn—it looks so old,
In truth, you'd find it hard to say
How it could ever have been young,
It looks so old and grey.
Not higher than a two years' child
It stands erect, this aged thorn

In fact, a number of critics feel that in trying to write poetry about simple things, in simple, unaffected language, Wordsworth exaggerated his intentions so much that he ended up by writing about things in childish language. To prove the point, the following two lines are quoted:

I've measured it from side to side
'Tis three feet long, and two feet wide.

Blank Verse

More than any other poet Wordsworth succeeded in bringing blank verse constructively close to the language of prose and speech without diminishing its poetic power. Deep human appeal in "Michael", moving reflectives in "Tintern Abbey" and numerous evocations of scenes instinct with feeling in *The Prelude* are communicated through this medium.

In spite of a few poetic expressions the style of the poem "Michael", keeps noticeably close to the language really used by men. The simplicity of language and action in "Michael" belongs to Wordsworth's own noble severity, warmed by his sharing of liberty, fraternity and equality with the shepherd.

The dialogue, which comprises about 125 lines of the poem, is the noblest that Wordsworth ever wrote. Written in blank verse of a rather stiff simplicity, much of it is straight narrative so unelaborated that it reads on the verge of the prosaic. "But the grave movement of the blank verse avoids the sudden slippery descents of some of the stanza poems. Equally it avoids the interspersed, detachable splendors and beauties that we find elsewhere, the obviously lovely lines and stanzas that stand out from passages of less intensity and make an immediate effect."[3] The poem presents dignified flow of sound and the tone of wise passiveness.

In "Tintern Abbey", Wordsworth has employed the double exposure technique which gives dramatic life to this philosophic lyric. It is quite unlike both lyrics and ballads in style; for its language is not simple by any standards, in it Wordsworth has not used the language of "the middle and lower classes of society". Words like "elevated", "sublime", "interfused", "genial", "ecstasy" and "zeal" are certainly not used by the Cumberland shepherd in his daily life. The syntax, too, is as far removed from ordinary conversation as the actual words. In "Tintern Abbey", we see what is often labelled the Miltonic' side of Wordsworth—the long involved sentences, the lofty emotions, and the grand manner. To Quote:

> *Here for the first time practically Wordsworth speaks the language that he was afterwards to speak in prose and in verse, in the tract on the Convention of Cintra as well as in The Prelude and The Excursion, in private letters and even in domestic conversation. With its long sentences, its involved grammar and its polysyllabic vocabulary it was a form of discourse that abandoned all pretence to being the poetry of the people. But it was a style that came much more easily to Wordsworth, sometimes indeed too easily,*

and it clearly expressed something fundamental in him that had hitherto been denied an outlet."[4]

"The Old Cumberland Beggar" partakes of Wordsworth's hard work to produce a sinewy but supple blank verse. This poem, though begun in 1797, was published in 1800. The opening clauses of its six verse paragraphs show something of its movement from a specious particularity of occasion, through a kind of drifting immediacy of impressions, on to an ending in baldly didactic generalizations.

The speciousness of particularly in the opening paragraph may be the result of Wordsworth's customary patching of pieces in blank verse; along with other passages finally excluded, the first three verse paragraphs may have been developed independently of each other before they were combined into a single poem.[5]

The Prelude containing fourteen books has an epic like structure and sublime expression. It bears a distinctly Miltonic tone. Wordsworth's style is sublime as it should be in an epic poem. He is indisputably the most sublime of our poets since Milton having the grandeur, austerity, sublimity in his poetry. *The Prelude* is a unique specimen of his poetic "grandeur" "austerity" and "sublimity" nothing is sublime unless it transports. As we see the uplifting power of the following lines:

. . . for there's not a man
That lives whose path not known his godlike hours,
And feels not what an empire we inherit
As natural beings in the strength of Nature,

(*The Prelude* III, 190-193)

In *The Prelude,* different kinds of blank verse, narrative, reflective, philosophical, rapturous exist together. *The Prelude* might be an autobiography but it is an autobiography of epic significance, sweep and stature. *The Prelude* is something unique in the literature of the world. It combines the epic power and range of poems like *The Divine Comedy, Paradise Lost* with the introspective voice of the writer himself. It bears several lofty utterances of Miltonic blank verse. There is no dearth of Miltonic similes like:

. . . stood alone
Beneath the sky, as if I had been born
On Indian plains, and from my mother's hut
Had run abroad in wantonness to sport
A naked savage, in the thunder shower.

Sonnets

In his long poetic career, Wordsworth wrote more than 500 sonnets. He revived the sonnet sequence, for the nineteenth century, after two centuries of somnolence. Within the sonnet's "narrow range", he composed a large number of sonnets with skill and seeming ease. He wrote several sonnets about sonnet, especially two in its direct defence. He regarded sonnet as a great form of poetry. He genuinely felt that those who were contemptuous of the sonnet were unable to appreciate its potentialities, so he implores the critic not to frown upon it:

Scorn not the Sonnet; Critic, you have frowned,
Mindless of its just honours;

Wordsworth's use of sonnet form is subjective, but hardly personal. In Elizabethan era, sonnet was a notable form of love lyric, but Wordsworth produced no love sonnets. His sonnets are divided in various groups—"Poems Dedicated to National Independence and Liberty and Order" (1802-10), "Sonnets Dedicated to Liberty and Order" (1831-45), "Sonnets upon the Punishment of Death" (1839-40), and the two ordered series, "The River Duddon" and "Ecclesiastical Sketches" and "Miscellaneous Sonnets".

The sonnet is divided into two forms—Petrarchan and Shakespearean, according to the rhyme scheme employed in it. The Petrarchan sonnet has two parts of eight and six lines respectively—the octave and sestet. The octave has two rhymes and the sestet has two or three rhymes different from those employed in the octave. The Shakespearean sonnet consists of three quatrains with alternate rhymes followed by one couplet. Wordsworth usually employed the Petrarchan form as used by Milton. He followed with little innovation Milton's practice of driving the sense past the line-endings, with the resultant run-on lines and heavy internal pauses. Milton tends to reverse the flow of thought, with question and answer or thesis or antithesis, so does Wordsworth. This reversal occurs, as in Milton's practice, immediately before or after the end of the octave rather than exactly at the end of the eighth line. "The World is too much with us" or the corollary sonnet, "Great Men Have Been among us" present this fact. Wordsworth's comments on the form of the sonnet cast a strong light on his practice. In 1833 he wrote to the scholar Alexander Dyce:

> *It would seem that the sonnet, like every other legitimate composition, ought to have a beginning, middle and an end; in other words, to consist of three parts, like the three propositions of a syllogism, if such an illustration may be used. But the frame of metre adopted by Italians does not accord with this view; and, as adhered to by them, it seems to be, if not arbitrary, best fitted to a division of the sense into two parts, of eight and six lines each. Milton, however, has not submitted to this; in the better half of his sonnets the sense does not close with the rhyme at the eighth line, but overflows into the second portion of the metre. Now, it has*

> *struck me that this is not done merely to gratify the ear by variety and freedom of sound, but also to aid in giving that pervading sense of intense unity in which the excellence of the sonnet has always seemed to me mainly to consist. Instead of looking at this composition as a piece of architecture, making a whole out of three parts, I have been much in the habit of preferring the image of an orbicular body— a sphere, or a dew drop.*[6]

The sonnets of 1802, taken as a group embody inevitably his reverence for the power of Nature and his scheme of reviving stored experience. He found in the sonnet a trumpet "to struggle through dark ways". The habit of looking at a subject from several perspectives produced thirty-four vignettes published in 1820 as *The River Duddon: A Series of Sonnets*. This series is like a loco-descriptive poem on the topography and vistas along the Duddon. Variations in mood and gnomic morality strung in quatorzains on the thread of the river can be taken sometimes objectively and sometimes metaphorically. The poet has made experimentation with the organic metaphor of a stream, "through a metaphor seemingly humble but not ultimately so, of the single-mindedness of the love-cycles that had earlier served poets' attempts to unify sonnets in a series".[7] His experimentation, resulting most of the way in modest achievement, culminates magnificently in the summarizing sonnet, entitled "After-thought":

> *I thought of Thee, my partner and my guide,*
> *As being past away. Vain sympathies!*
> *For, backward, Duddon! As I cast my eyes,*
> *I see what was, and is, and will abide;*
> *Still glides the Stream, and shall for ever glide:*
> *The form remains, the function never dies;*
> *While we, the brave, the mighty, and the wise,*
> *We men, who in our morn of youth defied*
> *The elements, must vanish; be it so!*

Enough, if something from our hands have power
To live, and act, and serve the future hour;
And if, as toward the silent tomb we go
Through love, through hope, and faith's transcendent dower,
We feel that we are greater than we know.

Here Wordsworth has concentrated on the oscillating pauses and shifting rhythms of blank verse. Rich mixtures of sound accompany the rhetorical figure of chiasmus, or crossed elements, in a rhymed poem.

Following the popularity of the Duddon sonnets, Wordsworth completed in 1821 the far more ambitious series of "Ecclesiastical Sonnets". In this series Wordsworth had the opportunity to enforce the coherence and proportion that had evaded his best efforts in ambitious blank verse. We need not end on a minor key. William Sharp was not absurd when he wrote in his introduction to *Sonnets of the Nineteenth Century* that "no poet of our own or any language could show ten sonnets equal in breadth of thought, verity of poetry, and beauty of expression to the ten greatest of Wordsworth".[8]

Other Forms of Poems: Lyric, Ode, Elegy

Wordsworth was highly praised for other genres of poetry also. He was highly original in odes and lyrics also. His "Resolution and Independence", "Ode to Duty", "She was a Phantom of Delight", "The Solitary Reaper", "I Wandered Lonely as a Cloud", "Elegiac Stanzas", "Intimations Ode", etc., are the most frequently anthologized poems in the language.

In "Resolution and Independence", Wordsworth has employed a style of perfect plainness. In fact it is a good example of Wordsworth's "profound simplicity". When we read the poem, we find many lines of extraordinary grandeur, but mingled with them are lines more pedestrian than could be found in an impressive poem from any other hand.

And, drawing to his side, to him did say,
This morning gives us promise of a glorious day.

In this poem, where Wordsworth adopts a form of the Spenserian stanza, he introduces a simile, which is a fine example of the modern handling of this classical type. It is the most characteristic of his greater lyrics.

One of the noblest poems in the whole range of English literature is Wordsworth's "Ode to Duty". This ode is on the model of Gray's "Ode to Adversity". Although a little strained both in language and sentiment, it is in its way a noble and dignified poem. To quote: "Gray and Horace are its models; it has, therefore, great majesty of sound, and is designed with much of the orderly and severe harmony that it celebrates. Wordsworth has forgotten his war against the eighteenth century diction, which here he uses with all his apostrophes, periphrases, antitheses and ceremonies; but the ending is that of a prosaic hymn. Few lyrics contain so many noble and proverbial sentences."[9]

With its simplicity, suggestiveness, pathos and verbal music, "The Solitary Reaper" remains a very delightful lyric. It illustrates Wordsworth's theory that simple and common words should be used in poetry. There are many suggestive lines and words in the poem. The lines of it are of the purest Romantic gold. They are: "For old, unhappy, far-off things. And battles long ago".

In contrast to earlier mentioned principle of Wordsworth's theory of language used in poetry, "Elegiac Stanzas" is a typically eighteenth century poem. Phrases like "thou rugged Pile", "merely silent Nature's breathing life", "this pageantry of fear", "chronicle of heaven", etc., can hardly find a place in ordinary man's language. But in absence of phrases like these, it would have been a poorer poem.

"The Immortality Ode" is essentially a free Pindaric poem of the type established by Cowley and perfected by Dryden. It is not an ode in repeated stanzas of a fixed form that is why Hazlitt remarked that in this ode, the Epode, the Strophe and the Antistrophe, he (Wordsworth) laughs to scorn. Its metrical structure is not uniform, but varies from line to line with the thought light or grave, accordingly as the sense is one or the other. The feet throughout is iambic. The lines vary in length from twelve syllables to the line with four feet. There is thus a "constant ebb and flow in the full tide of the song, but scarce two waves are alike". The majestic theme of the ode is matched by an equal majestic and sublime language. There is nothing of that "matter of factness" of which Coleridge complained about Wordsworth's poetry in general. Its tone is set in a usually lofty key. Saintsbury remarks, "Wordsworth puts his theories into his pockets and forgets about them." The stately words and diction used indicate the importance which the poet attached to the subject.

The cataracts blow their trumpets from the steep;
No more shall the grief of mine the seasons wrong,
I hear the Echoes through the mountains throng,
The winds come to me from the fields of sleep.

Passages, like the above mentioned can, by no stretch of imagination, be regarded as written in "a selection of language really used by men". There are, however, moments in which the poet says more than what he means, and loses himself in unaccustomed grandeur. Coleridge found fault with the seventh stanza of the Ode, and called it an instance of "mental bombast", i.e., "the use of thought and images too great for the subject".

But sound or unsound, sense or nonsense, it is poetry and magnificent poetry, from the first line to the last-poetry than which there is none better in any language, poetry such as there is not perhaps more than a small volume—full in all languages.[10]

Thus Wordsworth's contribution to English poetry and poetic diction is superb. In fact he ushered a new era in English poetry by his poetic diction. In any history of literature he must be awarded a pre-eminent place of honour and distinction.

References

1. Rai, D.V. and Mehrotra, R.R., *Literary Essays* (Part B), Bhartiya Vidya Prakashan, Varansi, p. 13.
2. *Ibid.*, pp. 14-15.
3. Hough, Graham, *The Romantic Poets,* Hutchinson's University Library, London, 1953, p. 47.
4. Batson, F.W, *Wordsworth: A Reinterpretation,* London Longmans, Green & Co. Ltd., 1954, pp. 142-43.
5. Woodring, Carl, *Wordsworth,* Harvard University Press, 1968, p. 55.
6. Dyce, Alexander, quoted in Carl Woodring, *Wordsworth,* pp. 161-62.
7. Woodring, Carl, *Wordsworth,* p. 174.
8. *Ibid.*, p. 178.
9. Elton, Oliver, *A Survey of English Literature 1780-1830,* Vol. II, Edward Arnold & Co. London, 1933, pp. 77-78.
10. Saintsbury, George, *A History of Nineteenth Century Literature,* Macmillan & Co. Ltd., London, 1925, p. 54.

14
Imagery

Imagery though a figure of speech related to vision, is broadly an expression evocative of an object of sensuous appeal. "It usually serves to make an impression more precise; it may, on the other hand, carry the mind from too close a dwelling on the original thought."[1] The purpose of an image is to intensify the feeling evoked with an idea.

Landscape Imagery

Wordsworth has employed landscape imagery in two ways—dark and light. Some poems use landscape as the vehicle of love and happiness while some present landscape as the vehicle of somber aspect of life. Wordsworth's earliest poems like "The Vale of Esthwaite" oscillate between landscape objectively described and landscape alive with horrors. In "Guilt and Sorrow", *The Borderers* and "Peter Bell", a somber landscape frames the action and even becomes a part of it. *The Borderers* is also grim in imagery, but Wordsworth's greatness lies in light description of landscape. The study of only one side, i.e., joy or sadness of landscape will be injustice to him. The study of Wordsworth's development of mind shows that the landscape is predominantly one of light, life and love in the middle period and darkness appears before and after.

Wordsworth's earliest poem, "The Vale of Esthwaite" has Miltonic echoes and Gothic extravagances. In this poem, landscape is objectively described and it is alive with horrors. The description which we find in this poem is a part of Wordsworth's poetry—"the mist clearing from the valley but still covering the lake and mountain tops, the shepherd's dog appearing and disappearing into the mist, the cottage smoking from the trees." The poem departs from the natural scene to one of "a cold and awful horror".

In "Guilt and Sorrow" and *The Borderers,* the landscape seems to objectify an inner world of guilt and failure in human sympathy but in "Peter Bell", the idea of redemption from evil appears though the landscape objectifies an inner state of mind. The landscape was never so desolate and bleak as can be seen in early poems, though the dark world that Wordsworth had seen was never to vanish entirely. Now landscape was not an objective correlative of an inner state of mind but an independent outer world as in *The Prelude,* landscape possesses an independent life which comes out to meet and act upon the mind.

In *The Prelude* I, we remember the "low breathings" and "sounds/of indistinguishable motion" that pursued the boy Wordsworth after he had stolen a bird from someone else' snare, and the peak "black and huge" that reared its head and towered between the boy in the stolen boat and the stars. From that encounter he carried

A dim and undermined sense
Of unknown modes of being; o'er my thoughts

There hung a darkness, call it solitude
Of blank assertion. No familiar shapes
Remained, no pleasant images of trees,
Of sea or sky, no colours of green fields;
But huge and mighty forms, that do not live
Like living men, moved slowly through the mind
By day, and were a trouble to my dream.

(*The Prelude* I, 392-400)

We find two different landscapes of darkness in Wordsworth. One is a clearly recognizable wasteland landscape that is the result of a failure in human sympathy. It signifies pride, apartness and guilt. The second may be called religious. "Whereas the wasteland landscape of guilt may be expected to vanish once Wordsworth's crisis had past, this second kind of darkness would seem to be more permanent."[2]

After long period of guilt and darkness comes the landscape drenched with light, overflowing with life, miraculous with love. In the "Anacron and Beauty" and "Moonlight", the poet presents landscape images to describe his beloved. As the vehicle of love and happiness, landscape proceeds with the landscape in "An Evening Walk" and in "Descriptive Sketches". In these poems, Wordsworth finds tranquility and religious awe in the landscape. In "An Evening Walk" it is "quiet" that leads the poet up the shady mountain brook and the evening scene composes and soothes him. The farewell light of day blends into night with religious awe and the poems ends with the "song of mountain streams" heard in the stillness of the evening air. In "Descriptive Sketches", religious note is more clearly heard through emphasis on liberty and freedom. The very fact that whole lines, which appear in the famous description of the Simplon Pass in Book VI of *The Prelude,* originally appeared in "Descriptive Sketches" would seem to point to the presence of religious intuition in "Descriptive Sketches".

> *. . . And sure there is a secret Power that reigns*
> *Here, where no trace of man the spot profanes,*

In "Tintern Abbey", Wordsworth uses landscape as the vehicle of the divine with such certainty and power that one feels totally unprepared for it by his previous poetry. The overall structure of the poem is built on the time pattern of human life set against the unchanging landscape. From the very beginning Wordsworth subtly idealizes the outer visible landscape to evoke a world alive with spirit in which man and nature are part of the same life. The steep, lofty cliffs along the bank of the Wye

> *On a wild secluded scene impress*
> *Thoughts of more deep seclusion; and connect*
> *The landscape with the quiet of the sky.*

Here Wordsworth directly links the visible scene with thoughts and at the same time suggests by "the quiet of the sky" the spiritual meaning that the landscape holds for him. Here human and natural merge together, for the orchard tufts with their unripe fruits, "Are clad in one green hue, and lose themselves/'Mid groves and copses".

Wordsworth merges forms and words together in one green hue and then emphasizes the silence and seclusion that one is prepared to deal with more than literal landscape. "The sweet sensations, the feelings of pleasure and the blessed mood in which one sees into the life of things rise in sequence from the purely organic to the merging once again of human and natural."[3] After some stanzas, the verse turns from the literal scene to its deeper significance. The literal, being minimized, the deeper significance finds human and natural in a spiritual union. "Wordsworth's imagery in "Tintern Abbey" tends to idealize, to harmonize, and to unify. His subject is the past, present and future significance of the scene that he beholds; as he dwells on the wild green landscape, human and natural blend into one idealized whole in which the one life lives and moves and has its being."[4]

After the *Lyrical Ballads of 1798*, landscape imagery of the purely happy sort decreases though it is present in some poems on "Naming of Places". In these poems places and persons are identified. "It was an April Morning" repeats most strongly the sense of landscape alive and active as a presence:

The spirit of enjoyment and desire
And hopes and wishes from all living things
Went circling, like a multitude of sounds.

Wordsworth identifies landscape with a person in the celebrated Lucy poems. Despite the numerous attempts of critics to identify Lucy with a real seems the living embodiment of English landscape.* She is the flower that grows on English ground, guarded by the "overseeing power" that kindles and restrains. In poems of 1800 volume, landscape lingers as indefinable presence. The volume of 1807 includes poems that have the sense of the radiant joyousness of the outer world and also poems that mark the loss of that sense. Helen Darbishire comments that this volume shows Wordsworth's returning again into himself after the ''effort of projection" of the *Lyrical Ballads.*[5] In the poem "To a Skylark", the poet resolves to share the lark's joy, he nevertheless pictures himself as plodding on. "Resolution and Independence" describes as perfect a day as one could hope to have, with the sun shining after the night's rain and the birds singing in distant woods:

All things that love the sun are out of doors;
The sky rejoices in the morning's birth;
The grass is bright with rain-drops;-on the moors

But the poet himself falls from joy to melancholy, "Dim sadness—and blind thoughts" (Stanza II). The world is too much with us and Wordsworth himself is forlorn, feeling unresponsive to winds and sea.

The real end of the landscape of light comes, of course, with the "Intimation Ode". There the celestial light, the glory and the dream, fade not to darkness but to the light of common day as the prison of the self closes in upon the growing child. Now landscape, as living body of the divine closes to be a significant vehicle in Wordsworth's poetry and its place is taken by landscape structures. Landscape imagery in *The Excursion* is not much effective. In "Tintern Abbey", the landscape speaks of the abiding presence that rolls through all things, but in *The Excursion* it gives "shadowy intimations".

Of purpose akin to those of man
But wrought with mightier arm than new prevails.

In the landscape of *The Excursion,* life increasingly departs.

Thus it can be said that landscape objectifies the psychic world. In "Guilt and Sorrow", landscape provides a natural symbol for immanent divinity. In *The Prelude,* landscape combines both these functions. But in *The Excursion,* the landscape images seem like set pieces. In fact, Wordsworth's later poetry loses the light aspect in landscape.

Water Imagery

Wordsworth has used water imagery in all its aspects—its sounds and quiet, its movements and its peace, its transparency and its power to reflect. In his first water poem—"Lines Written Near Richmond", upon the Thames at Evening—the poet describes the gloom that may overtake the hopes of the poet by describing the darkness of the stream behind the boat. He wishes that the quiet movement of the water may lead the mind to flow in equal quiet. Wordsworth's thoughts move between the actual stream and the mind; as the poem progresses, he comes closer and closer to see the mind in the water scene. In the analogy, the poet's hopes are the center of interest. The water lingers as vehicle. Wordsworth, next, turns to the mind:

O glide! Fair stream! For ever so,
Thy quiet soul on all bestowing,
Till all our minds for ever flow
As thy deep waters now are flowing.

There is attraction between the river and the mind—the mind is to flow—but the mind is not yet altogether seen in the water. Finally, in

Vain thoughts!—Yet be as now thou art
That in thy waters may be seen
The image of a poet's heart,
How bright, how solemn, how serene!

In *The Prelude*, Wordsworth writes of his own life and constantly draws on water imagery. Water provides images for the mind and its powers, for the imagination and for poetry. Water metaphors gain in significance and weight from the presence of so much actual water. The recurrent water metaphors lend weight to the water symbol of the great climatic scene on Mount Snowdon. Here, literal and metaphoric waters hold together. The poet on the mountain, looks over the moonlit sea of mist covering the surrounding hills and hearing from a distant chasm the roar of waters:

The universal spectacle throughout
Was shaped for admiration and delight.
Grand in itself alone, but in that breach
Through which the homeless voice of waters rose,

That dark deep thoroughfare had Nature lodg'd
The soul, the Imagination of the Whole.

Here the voice is virtually the voice of God. The recurrent water metaphors present the movement of the poem as a whole. In the last book of *the Prelude,* water stands for the life stream of consciousness in the mind. In the beginning of *The Prelude,* the music of poetry has been presented by the ceaseless music of the river Derwent while in the end water unites poetry and imagination and poet.

The River Duddon, on one level, seems almost the reverse of *The Prelude.* In *The Prelude,* Wordsworth writes of his own life and constantly draws on water imagery. River Duddon is directly about a river and indirectly about Wordsworth himself. The Duddon's function, "O heal and to restore / to soothe and cleanse, not madden and pollute!" sounds remarkably like Wordsworth's own ideal for himself as a poet. The image of the river's birth and growth is parallel to birth and growth of human life in general. The river is a "child of the clouds" whose foster mother is the earth; it is a "cradled Nursling" with a clear voice which grows into "a Brook of loud and stately march". The imagery of the union of the river and its tributary stream signifies human marriage and the river's advance to the sea suggests the mingling of the soul with eternity:

Still glides the Stream, and shall for ever glide;
The Form remains, the Function never dies;-
While we, the brave, the mighty, and the wise,
We Men, who in our morn of youth defied
The elements, must vanish; be it so!

(The River Duddon, After-thought, XXXIV)

Water images abound, of course, outside *The Prelude* and The River Duddon but elsewhere they are less central. Water appears as a vehicle for the current of emotion, for the streams of life and time and for the streams of liberty and religion. Water is a natural image for emotion and since feeling is basic to life and equally natural image for life itself. Wordsworth's strong sense of life in water perhaps helps to account for the central position of water in *The Prelude.* The sound of water is the voice of the landscape and the voices of mountain torrents and of the ocean is the music of liberty. In the "Ecclesiastical Sonnets", Wordsworth uses water imagery for the development of the church. Here water is not actually mentioned but it sounds as an undercurrent.

Thus water is one of Wordsworth's most frequently employed vehicles. Literal River is reinforced by metaphor and simile, so that symbolic values become clear. Water imagery is dominant in *The Prelude* but sounds faintly in *The Excursion.* It is focal in "The River Duddon" but provides a frame of reference for the "Ecclesiastical Sonnets". In the beginning, it is subjective but it becomes an external image and objective reality by the time of "Ecclesiastical Sonnets". "The suitability of water as an image for the life of the mind since it suggests the substantial character of thought and the union of thought and thing thought of. Even more basically, I think, water images life and links life with feeling; to live is to feel, and while the currents of feelings flow freely in the mind the stream of poetry and life run freely too."[6]

Sounds

Wordsworth uses several objects as a part of landscape. Though the voices that sound in the landscape exist like the landscape itself, they have their own value and must be regarded as themselves things. Both sounds and silence attracted Wordsworth. Sounds speak of life, its horror, joy, anguish and mystery; silence speaks of the unknown and of peace. When sounds fade away into silence, both symbolize the mysterious and invisible.

In Wordsworthian landscape human sounds are often sad. Orpheus sings "his tale of sorrows o'er" and the cottage woman sings "a plaintive sad" lullaby to her child. Human sounds in "An Evening Walk" are distant and faintly heard. They are clearer in "Descriptive Sketches" but are for the most part lost among the sounds of nature. Wordsworth's women are mostly sufferers and their voice indicates solitary anguish. Even the song of Solitary Reaper is melancholic. A human voice of joy is rare. Dorothy's voice "was like hidden Bird that sang"; in Wordsworth's worst crisis, "like a brook/ that did but cross a lonely road", she was able to restore him to himself. The idiot boy's joyous burring and the mirth of the idle shepherd boys are the only completely happy human voices. It may be due to certain distaste for normal human noise. Wordsworth dislikes noise, crowded city and streets. The proportion of human sound is small in the landscape. What stirs Wordsworth is the natural song of life that rose from all living things:

Beast and bird, the lamb,
The shepherd's dog, the linnet and the thrush,
Vied with this waterfall, and made a song
Which, while I listened, seemed like the wild growth
Or like some natural produce of the air,
That could not cease to be.

(It was an April Morning: Fresh and Clear II, 25-30)

The lark's is a more constant sound. Its song is a note of joy contrasting with human "labour and grief and solitude and fear". The nightingale mourns or pours out a song of fiery passion, and the poet prefers the stock dove's pensive song of love and serious faith. The thrush's note is one of enchantment: it summons up for poor Susan a vision of home; it summons the poet out into the rain and wind to sing along with it. Wordsworth likes the cuckoo most. The thrilling voice whose bodily source remains unseen calls up for the poet an equally unsubstantial world, the golden time of youth when the poet was full of youth. Years later, the cuckoo had still its prophetic power, "wandering in solitude, and evermore / Foretelling and Proclaiming". Bird song and the sound of the wind are free from human limitations and have invisibility of the source of the sound.

Admonishing the man who walks below
Of solitude, and silence in the sky.

So they fascinated Wordsworth very much. The sound of the wind, always invisible in source leads even more directly to the "visionary power". The power of sound can "breathe an elevated mood, by form/or image unprofaned"; from such moods of "shadowy exultation" Wordsworth "retains an obscure sense/possible sublimity".

Echoes too touch the ear with "visionary impulses" and lead to thoughts of another world. He clears it in "On the Power of Sound", where he links the power of music with reason, finding in the harmonies of music earthly evidence of a divine art. He still heard all sounds as part of a universal harmony.

All worlds, all natures, mood and measure keep
For praise and ceaseless gratulation, poured
Into the ear of God, their Lord!

Sometimes Wordsworth uses silence to express himself as silence is the best language of the spirit. The voiceless glowworm shining beneath the ferns summoned Wordsworth to continue *The Prelude* just as the music of the redbreasts had:

Silence touched me here
No less than sound had done before

(*The Prelude* VII, 36-37)

Silence and sound alike lead to some thing other than themselves.

Architectural Structures

Wordsworth in many poems employed architectural structures. In the beginning, his structures are mostly ruined, as the ruin of Stonehenge in "Guilt and Sorrow" and the ruined castle and deserted chapel of *The Borderers*. After the early poems, man's violence and destructiveness recede into the background. Later structures which Wordsworth describes are mostly religious structures. The religious structure in its first appearance is also ruined. One of the most terrible images in Wordsworth is that of the deserted chapel on the rocks in *The Borderers*. The period of *The Lyrical Ballads, The Prelude* and the *Poems of 1807* offers little by way of concrete structures. The religious structure is a frequent vehicle in the poetry that followed *The Excursion*.

> *Ruined structure, domestic structure, religious structure—the architectural image moves between the poles of mutability and permanence and as domestic structure images the life of man.*[7]

Architectural images are not usually dominant images, except in *The Excursion*. The ruin of the Norton mansion presents the images of the perishable things of man set against the imperishable things of the spirit. In the "Ecclesiastical Sonnets", metaphorical river and literal religious structure combine to image the imperishable. Thus architectural images appear throughout the entire range of Wordsworth's poetry. The early architectural images link desolation and decay with man's imperfection; the later architectural images make of nature and man temples of the spirit. Though architectural images are by nature static, they have less life.

People

Wordsworth's figures move through the Wordsworthian landscape. In fact, most of them have emanated from the landscape itself. These figures are clearly recognizable as they are elemental and enduring, suffering and solitary. Wordsworth portrays the figures of the child, the young girl, the joyous irresponsible, the suffering woman, the enduring old man. Some are solitaries and some are wanderers.

The most significant image that Wordsworth portrays is that of the child, though it appears neither in Wordsworth's early poetry, nor in poetry after 1807. However, Wordsworth's interest in the child seems threefold. Primarily there is the figure that belonged to memory, the child William, and then there are actual children whose psychology interested Wordsworth. Most important, there is the life of spirit to which the child is a supreme symbol. In his early poetry, Wordsworth presents child only in "Guilt and Sorrow". Here the father mercilessly beats the child. Perhaps as image of undeserved suffering the child fails to develop, but as an agent of redemption, however, the child persists. Wordsworth's interest in William helped him to regain the hiding places of his power, the wellsprings of his being, when he was uncertain of his power. William was to the man Wordsworth the way back into creative power. Speaking of William's early love of reading and its strengthening of imaginative life, Wordsworth remarks:

Dumb yearnings, hidden appetites, are ours,
And they must have their food, Our childhood sits,
Our simple childhood, sits upon a throne
That hath more power than all the elements.

I guess not what this tells of Being past,
Nor what it augurs of the life to come.

In *The Prelude* II (232-65), we find the infant Babe, responsive to his mother's love and possessing the "first/ poetic spirit of our human life". Leavis connects the babe with "Tintern Abbey" and Lionel Trilling with the "Intimation Ode". According to Leavis, Wordsworth in *The Prelude* passage "is explaining how he comes to have the kind of experience he describes in 'Tintern Abbey'."[8] Trilling finds that "the first affections" for which the poet gives the thanks in the Ode are the affections that lead the child to perceive objects not merely as objects but "as objects-and-judgements, as valued objects", to perceive "in short, with glory".[9] Both critics have evidently recognized in the child Wordsworth's image for the creative life of the mind.

In "Intimation Ode" Wordsworth describes the child part symbol, part reality. This ode uses child image from stanza V to IX. In V stanza he has the notion that in our childhood we are surrounded by the glory of heaven. In stanza VI the poet holds the child image steadily. Now earth provides the new born child with all kinds of pleasures to amuse him and to make him forget about the heavenly home he comes from. stanza VII renews the image of the actual child—living and playing child but the concluding lines, "As if his whole vocation. Were endless imitation" reminds us that the child has another and more real vocation, the spiritual. Then in stanza IX, Wordsworth develops child symbol without losing contact with reality. In his soul's immensity the little child lives in his own world, not yet yoked by custom and tradition. He possesses intuitive knowledge of truths that the adults he lives among have long lost sight of and must struggle to regain. The Dear Child of "It is a beauteous evening" and the little cottage girl of "We Are Seven" both are specific examples of Wordsworth's statement here: young Caroline can play happily without solemn thought, her nature being innately divine; the cottage child sings with confidence to her brother and sister who lie in the graveyard. "Set against the darkness in which the adults have lost their knowledge of spiritual truths, the darkness of the grave, the little child stands glorious on his being's height. Immortality broods over him like the arching sky visible as a presence."[10]

In *The Excursion*, we meet Solitary comforting a little child as if Wordsworth had contemplated a further development of the child as instrument of redemption. The child who lives in the heart was apparently to open the way to spiritual rebirth—once again the child is part actual, part memory, part symbol.

The II figure, that is, of the young girl appears to a limited extent in Wordsworth's early and late poetry of 1798-1807, like the image of the child. In earlier poetry, he uses landscape imagery to describe the person of the poet's beloved. In fact, Wordsworth's loveliest girls are nature's children as Lucy, the Highland Girl and the Solitary Reaper. "The Three Cottage Girls", paying tribute to the Highland Girl, presents the image in a new manner. The Italian maid glitters like a star; the Helvetian's beauty "dazzles the thick wood" but the Highland Girl really seems a "Bright Star". One by one the three girls are praised as possible brides—Edith with regal imagery, Dora as nature's child and Sara with imagery from the skies. In order to present life, Wordsworth presents child and young girl who belong to the landscape of love, light and joy.

The III figure, the joyous irresponsible is also Wordsworth's mighty affirmation of life. Idiot boy, beggars, thieves idle shepherd boys, drunken waggoner, etc., have also been employed by Wordsworth, as manifestation of the joy of living, however, lowly. Wordsworth himself seems intoxicated by Johnny's mindless pleasure as he protests to their muses against his inability to relate "But half of what to him Befell." The old Cumberland beggar who plies his weary journey "Bow bent his eyes for ever on the ground" is, of course, scarcely a manifestation of either life or joy. The other beggars, the imposing womanlike an Amazonian queen and the rascally boys with the flowers around their hats clearly delight the poet by their physical beauty and irrepressible activity.

Just as Wordsworth presented two aspects of landscape, similarly his people also fall into two categories. People presenting joy of life have already been presented. Now there is a description of people representing suffering. The IV figure, the suffering woman belongs primarily to the dark landscape. The figure in its earliest form is one of undeserved suffering and innocence; as the pattern develops, some of the women suffer the shame of bearing illegitimate children; some simply endure their suffering, some break under suffering and some are purified by it. The Female Vagarant, Margaret of "The Ruined Cottage" and Idonea of "The Borderers" suffer woes not of their own making but the injustice of social conditions afflicts them. Their suffering is "permanent, obscure and dark. /And has the nature of infinity". Ruth and Emily Norton are completely innocent suffers, though darkness in their case is relieved to some extent. Ruth's trouble is deep rooted, having its origin in her neglected childhood. But in her childhood she had run free over hill and dale, piping on her pipe of straw,

Had built a bower upon the green,
As if she from her birth had been
An infant of the woods.

When the gay, handsome youth from Georgia deserts her after their marriage, she goes mad. Eventually she escapes from her prison and returns to the fields and woods that in her childhood had almost been her home. Her regression to her childhood way mitigates her sufferings as the suffering of the Female Vagrant or of Margaret is never mitigated. Like Ruth, Emily Norton withdraws into religion. When we first meet Emily after the death of father and brothers, she already is carrying "inward a serene and perfect sway", her grief subjected to a holy "Though stern and rigorous, melancholy!" After the white doe has reappeared to share Emily's solitude, Emily's gloom is lightened so that she is "forlorn, but not disconsolate" and able to return from "the Abyss. . . . Of Thought" without grief and pain.

The Female Vagrant, Margaret, Ruth and Emily Norton are essentially solitary figures. The figure of woman and child follows much the same development from unrelieved suffering to suffering tempered by religion. The unhappy woman of "An Evening Walk", the Grison gypsy of "Descriptive Sketches", Martha Ray of "The Thorn", the mad mother of "Her Eyes are Wild"—all are figures of suffering. They have the nature of infinity. Their stories can be summed up in the doleful cry that Martha cries at all times and seasons:

Oh misery! Oh misery!
Oh Woe is me! Oh Misery!

But the story of Ellen in *The Excursion*, while equally unhappy, is a story to which "religious tenderness of heart, / Grieving for sin" lends sanctity. In some poems, the figure of the deserted woman is linked to the purely maternal figure as we see in "A Forsaken Indian Woman", "The Sailor's Mother", "The Emigrant Mother", "The Force of Prayer", "The Affliction of Margaret", etc. The sufferings of deserted women present much of human predicament. The theme of desertion in Wordsworth is connected with his treatment of Annette Vallon. It seems worth observing that the sense of having been deserted was part of Wordsworth's own experience, when he suffered endless nightmares in consequences of the atrocities accompanying the French Revolution. The figure of the suffering woman belongs to this darkness, this death like sense of desertion in the soul.

The other major figure who embodies the human predicament is the old man. He first appears in "Juvenilia, No. XV, Fragment of a "Gothic Tale". Blind and helpless, the old man clearly prefigures the Baron Herbert of "The Borderers". Herbert's figure in many ways sums up the helplessness of man. Blind, aged, palsied, dependent on the kindness of others, Herbert is deserted, not once but twice. The helplessness of man appears even more clearly in the figure of the blind beggar of *The Prelude*. Once in a London crowd Wordsworth watched the faces of the passers-by with a sense of the mystery of other lives. Far travelled in this mood, suddenly he saw the blind beggar,

Who, with upright face,
Stood, propped against a wall, upon his chest
Wearing a written paper, to explain
His story, whence he came and who he was.

Caught by the spectacle, Wordsworth was stunned. He stood and gazed "As if admonished from another world." Herbert's figure also connects with the ghostly soldier of *The Prelude* who seems the embodiment of solitude. Unlike Herbert, the soldier is alone, with neither dog nor staff; the desolation and simplicity of his very dress "seem'd akin to solitude".

The old man of "Resolution and Independence" also presents the uncanniness of these old men, the sense of an apparition from another world. Then the leech-gatherer appears to the despondent poet "the oldest man . . . that ever wore grey hairs, a figure who in his old age embodies not man's helplessness but man's power to endure". Matthew, Simon Lee and Timothy of "The Childless Father" are human figures—they have a quiet acceptance of decay and loss without the sublimity of some of Wordsworth's other old men.

The character of the Wanderer in *The Excursion* seems an image of idealized perfection. Wordsworth draws in him a figure of love and wisdom unblemished by human failing. Unlike other old men, both the Wanderer and the Solitary of *The Excursion* lack something. The Wanderer, although idealized, is most satisfactory in the passages of Book I in which he seems as a solitary figure, watching the hills grow larger in the darkness, watching the world at sunrise lie before him in gladness. "The solitary Wanderer seems to be Wordsworth's central image for the human being: when the Solitary does not wander and the Wanderer ceases to be solitary, the vision seems to be disintegrating."[11]

Taken collectively, the Wordsworth human—child, young girl, joyous irresponsible, suffering woman and enduring old man-emerges as a figure with distinct limitations. But regardless of these limitations, they are the vehicle of an impressive vision. This vision includes something beyond both human predicament and human achievement.

References

1. *Dictionary of Literary Terms* (ed.), Thomas T. Shipley, p. 156.

2. Marsh, Florence, *Wordsworth's Imagery: A Study in Poetic Vision*, p. 37.

3. *Ibid.*, p. 4.

4. *Ibid.*, p. 42.

5. "Introduction", *Wordsworth's Poems in Two Volumes,* 1807 (ed.), Helen Darbishire, p. xL

6. Marsh, Florence, *Wordsworth's Imagery: A Study in Poetic Vision,* p. 96.

7. *Ibid.*, p. 101.

8. Leavis, "Wordsworth", in *Revaluation: Tradition and Development in English Poetry*, pp. 161-62.

9. Trilling, Lionel, "The Immortality Ode", in *The Liberal Imagination: Essays in Literature and Society*, New York, Viking Press, 1950, p. 145.

10. Marsh, Florence, *Wordsworth's Imagery: A Study in Poetic Vision*, p. 68.

11. *Ibid.*, p. 83.

* Lucy has been variously identified as Mary "Hutchinson, Dorothy, Lucy Gray, Hartley Coleridge, etc., Both Arthur Beatty, in Wordsworth: Representative poems ed. Arthur Beatty (Garden City, Doubleday, Doran, 1937), p. 318, and Herbert Hartman, in "Wordsworth's 'Lucy Poems,'" PMLA, 49(1934), 134-42, remind us that the name "Lucy" was a common place in Eighteenth century elegiac poems. If Lucy had a human counterpart it was in Dorothy.

15

Symbolism

Symbol is a very significant means to express the reality—the visible world as well as the invisible. The symbols penetrate the surface reality and suggest and evoke what language ordinarily cannot. In modern times there has been a great emphasis on the use of symbols. Virginia Woolf, in her essay "On Not Knowing Greek", stresses "the function of symbol to enhance the importance of what it symbolizes."[1]

Landscape Symbol

Wordsworth has employed landscape as the vehicle of his thought. Landscape has been used as a symbol of various thoughts and feelings. In his earliest poetry, landscape is a vehicle of fear. In "The Vale of Esthwaite" the landscape is alive with horrors. Again in "Guilt and Sorrow", "The Borderers" and "Peter Bell", a serious landscape frames the action. In "Peter Bell", the landscape stanzas are made to symbolize and objectify the sailor's inner landscape. "Salisbury Plain" stands as the outer symbol of desolation wandering on in the wind. The sailor comes to the desolate structure the pile of Stonehenge which is a symbol of terror and misery.

The symbolic use of landscape in "The Borderers" to reinforce action has been more generally recognized. Here, Marmaduke, the protagonist, is not guilty from the beginning but stands at first between Oswald, the embodiment of the cold unfeeling reason and of blind old man, whose suffering should elicit compassionate aid. The landscape in the beginning has no great significance but when the scene shifts to half ruined castle—desolate structure, the use of landscape to reinforce action becomes clear. The desolate prospect of the scene in which Herbert sinks exhausted, the deserted chapel on the rocks, whose bell ringing in the wind has drawn Herbert to it hoping to find help, seem to symbolize the state of man when natural feelings have been cut off and only the hard rock of intellect and pride is left. Oswald's story of his own experience thereafter told to Marmaduke, when he was led by his crew to abandon their captain on a bare rock having no grass, no shade, repeats the symbol. In "Guilt and Sorrow" and "The Borderers", the landscape seems to symbolize an inner world of guilt and of failure in human sympathy.

"Not content to let the symbolism of landscape speak for itself, Wordsworth cautions the stranger who reads his lines to remember that "he who feels contempt/For any living thing" is failing to mature, that "true knowledge to love."[2] Landscape is not only the symbol of terror, guilt, sorrow or tension; it is also a symbol of love and happiness. In "An Evening Walk" and in "Descriptive Sketches", landscape is the sole companion for the poet's departed pleasures. In "An Evening Walk", it is "quiet" that leads the poet up the shady mountain brook and the evening scene composes and soothes him. Wordsworth uses landscape as the vehicle of the divine with certainty and power in "Tintern Abbey". The overall structure of the poem is built on the time pattern of human life set against the unchanging landscape. "Tintern Abbey" primarily presents the landscape as the abiding symbol of one life and so belongs to the pattern of life and love. The landscape, by virtue of its unchanging and enfolding quality symbolizes the living presence of the divine. The sheepfold stands as the symbol of Michael's sorrow and endurance. Michael himself in his strong old age seems akin to the rocks and sun and clouds, elemental like the sheep and land he loves. The thorn is gray and leafless. Like the stone pile, it belongs to the wasteland group of symbols; though alive it is a dead thing. The thorn is simply a wretched thing overgrown like a rock with lichens. It clearly intends to stand as a comparable symbol for Martha Ray's misery. "Set against it as a life symbol is the beauteous heap of moss with its lovely colours that seems to represent nature's healing powers."[3] Martha Ray herself, who in her scarlet cloak sits beside the thorn

When the blue daylight's in the skies,
And when the whirlwind's on the hill,
Or frosty air is keen and still.

(The Thorn, 72-74)

"The Brothers" is a tale of sorrow like "Michael" but it is in a way exactly opposite of "Michael". Michael's love of the land helps him endure the grief of his son's shame; whereas to Leonard, the sorrow of his brother's death makes valley he had loved "a place in which he could not bear to live". Here we find negative symbols. Leonard through his long absence at sea had dreamed of home, visualizing the mountains and "the forms of sheep that grazed / on verdant hills-with dwelling among trees", and shepherds clad in the country gray. Nevertheless to him, the forms of the mountains in the end are not sufficient comfort. Here, life symbols yield to eternity symbols. The Brothers perhaps relate more nearly to the later books of *The Excursion* than to the poems in which the divine life exists here and now.

Wordsworth has a habit of identifying landscape with a person. This is present in the celebrated Lucy Poems. Despite the numerous attempts of critics to identify her Lucy seems the living symbol of English landscape. She is the flower that grows on English ground guarded by the "overseeing power that kindles or restrains". The poem "Resolution and Independence" deals, of course, with a progression of moods—the blithe unthinking happiness, the blind thoughts and dim sadness, and the resolution of fear and dejection into a mood of self-laughter and independence of mind. Here the leech-gatherer is a unifying symbol who in his old age is like a rock and manifests human ability to endure. Landscape in *The Excursion* is an arbitrary and unnatural symbol of transcendent divinity where landscape in "Guilt and Sorrow" successfully symbolizes the psychic world; landscape in "Tintern Abbey" successfully provides a natural symbol for immanent divinity; landscape in *The Prelude* combines both these functions, but landscape seems ill-adapted to convey:

> *The measures and the forms*
> *Which an abstract intelligence supplies;*
> *Whose kingdom is, where time and space are not.*
>
> (*The Excursion* IV, 74-76)

"The White Doe" also seems to have reconciling symbol. In the figure of white doe, Wordsworth unites the healing power of nature with that of spiritual grace. From the moment of its first appearance, the white doe is more than natural. White as a lily, beauteous as the moon, in a cloudless sky or a single ship glittering in sunlight, the doe is so bright that it is uncertain whether she is a truly forest creature.

Or a Spirit for one day given,
A pledge of grace from purest heaven.

The doe is so successfully spiritualized so apart from her own kind, that she seems unreal. The white doe in its white radiance is a symbol of eternity. It has so little animality that it seems supernatural more than natural. Like the landscape in "Tintern Abbey", the white doe is idealized so that the natural rises into the spiritual so that the natural is spiritual. The weeds and spear grass of "The Ruined Cottage" are a natural symbol both of desolation and decay and of the life of nature.

Child as a Symbol

Wordsworth's child is not always a reality. Sometimes he makes a symbolic use of child. First, child appears as a symbol in "Guilt and Sorrow" as symbol of indwelling life. In "Intimation Ode" child is a symbol of immanent divinity. Wordsworth traces the growth of man, with the attendant loss of the freshness of the world. Child is present in both ways—physically and symbolically. Physical child grows into a man but the spiritual child is the symbol of the soul. In *The Prelude,* the child is a symbol of indwelling life.

Like child, Wordsworth has presented young girls as symbol of life. Wordsworth's loveliest girls—Lucy Gray, Highland Girl, Solitary Reaper are all nature's children, almost embodiments of the landscape.

Water as a Symbol

In *The Prelude,* water as a symbol appears again and again. This symbol has been used in the sense of recurrent and central metaphor. Water provides images for the mind and its powers for the imagination and for poetry. There is so much actual water in the poet's description of various places. The presence of so much water provides weight to the water symbol.

In the beginning of *The Prelude,* the ceaseless music of the river Derwent symbolizes the music of poetry. While in the last (XIV) book water symbolizes the recurrent water metaphors for the movement of the poem as a whole for the life stream of a human being and for the stream of consciousness in the mind. When the poet describes a scene on the mountain, looking over mist covering the surrounding hills and hearing from a distant chasm the roar of waters:

The universal spectacle throughout
Was shaped for admiration and delight.
Grand in itself alone, but in that breach
Through which the homeless voice of waters rose,
That dark deep thorough had Nature lodg'd
The Soul, the Imagination of the Whole.

(*The Prelude* XIII, 60-65)

The voice that issues from the dark abyss is here virtually the voice of God: the scene itself is the "image of a mighty mind" and the voices that issue forth "to silent light" are in the early version the divine under presence in one's own soul and in later version "recognitions of transcendent power". "The recurrent water metaphors for the movement of the poem as a whole, for the life stream of a human being, and for the stream of consciousness in the mind are drawn together in the water symbol of the last book of *The Prelude.*"[4] In fact, the river Derwent which symbolizes the music of poetry in the beginning unites poetry and imagination and poet in the end. In *The Prelude,* Wordsworth constantly uses water symbol to write of his own life.

"The River Duddon" though directly about a river, symbolizes Wordsworth himself. The Duddon's function, "to heal and to restore / To soothe and cleanse, not madden and pollute" (VIII, 13-14) sounds remarkably like Wordsworth's own ideal for himself as a poet. Again in XIIth sonnet, the river's "Bright liquid mansions" which endure when "the solidities of mortal pride" have crumbled, remind one of the mansion of verse that is also a transparent veil. We may not insist on this particular symbolism but certainly there lies behind the image of the river's birth and growth the parallel birth and growth of human life in general. The union of the river and its tributary stream symbolizes human marriage and the river's advance to the sea suggests the mingling of the soul with eternity.

. . . to advance like Thee;
Prepared, in peace of heart, in calm of mind
And soul, to mingle with Eternity!

(The River Duddon, XXXIII, 12-14)

The river is an immutability symbol because like man it is born and grows but unlike man it does not pass away. Though "the solidities of mortal pride/ Palace and tower are crumbled to dust" (XII, 9-10), the river flows on. Human life seen against the permanence of nature is transitory.

Still glides the Stream, and shall for ever glide;
The Form remains, the Function never dies;
While we, the brave, the mighty, and the wise,
We Men, who in our morn of youth defied
The elements, must vanish; be it so!

(The River Duddon, XXXIV, 5-9)

The sonnet, "Brook! Whose Society the Poet Seeks" makes water a pure life symbol altogether divorced from human nature. Wordsworth's strong sense of life in water perhaps helps to account for the central position of water in *The Prelude*. In "The Longest Day" time like life is a river and the sea to which it flows is of course eternity. The Mighty Being of "It is a beauteous evening, calm and free" links ocean and the divine.

Sounds as a Symbol

Sound also comes in the category of major symbols. The voices that sound in the landscape exist like the landscape itself primarily as symbols. Sounds in Wordsworthian landscape do have symbolic value and must be regarded as themselves things. Wordsworth was attracted towards sounds and silence. Whereas sounds symbolize life and its terror, joy, anguish, and mystery; silence speaks of the unknown and of peace. As sounds fade away into silence, both symbolize the mysterious and invisible.

Wordsworth had certain distaste for normal human noise. Not only does he dislike personal talk and neighbourly gossip, he dislikes crowded city streets and noise and confusion. The music that did stir Wordsworth was the natural song of life that rose from all living things:

Beast and bird, the lamb,
The shepherd's dog, the linnet and the thrush,
Vied with this waterfall, and made a song
Which, while I listened, seemed like the wild growth
Or like some natural produce of the air,
That could not cease to be.

(It was an April Morning; Fresh and Clear II 25-30)

The song of lark, nightingale and thrush are inspiring to the poet. The song of lark is a note of joy contrasting with human "labour and grief and solitude and fear". The nightingale pours out a song of fiery passion and the poet prefers the stock dove's pensive song of love and serious faith. The thrush's song has a note of enchantment. It summons for poor Susan a vision of home. It summons the poet out into the wind and rain to sing along with it. Its song provides a symbol of the poet's own. It is a "wandering voice", invisible and mysterious. The cuckoo is Wordsworth's favourite bird. The cuckoo's bodily presence remains unseen but the thrilling voice calls up for the poet an equally unsubstantial world and the golden time of youth when the poet was full of hope.

The sound of the wind, always invisible in source symbolizes the "visionary power". The poet calls the wind "ghostly language of the ancient earth", a "strange utterance" that makes the sky and the motion of the clouds mysterious. The power of sound can "breathe an elevated mood, by form/ or image unprofaned".

Echoes too touch the ear with "visionary impulses" and lead to thoughts of another world. The poem "On the Power of Sound" expresses clearly the power of sound suggesting the invisible. Wordsworth links the power of music with reason, finding in the harmonies of music earthly evidence of a divine art. He believes:

By one pervading spirit
Of tones and numbers all things are controlled,
He still heard all sounds as part of a universal harmony;
All worlds, all natures, mood and measure keep
For praise and ceaseless gratulation, poured
Into the ear of God, their Lord!

(On the Power of Sound)

Even more than sound, silence has been used as the symbol of the spiritual. Silence is the best language of the spirit. The voiceless glowworm shining beneath the ferns summoned Wordsworth to continue *The Prelude* just as the music of the redbreasts had; Silence touched me here. No less than sound had done before. The language of the twin peaks that speak to the Solitary, in addition to the sounds wind and water, includes

Music of finer tone; a harmony,
So do, I call it, though it be the hand
Of silence, though there be no voice;-the clouds,
The mist, the shadows, light of golden suns,
Motion of moonlight, all come thither-touch,
And have an answer-thither come and shape
A language not unwelcome to sick hearts.

(*The Excursion* II, 710-16)

The most characteristic sound that Wordsworth uses as symbol is the sound of water, discussed above.

Architectural Symbols

Architectural metaphors and similes like water metaphors and similes reinforce and make explicit the architectural symbols. Mansions and temples are the kinds of structures that appear most frequently. These structures symbolize permanence more often than mutability. Religious structures, especially the church symbolize the permanence. Against the impermanence of human existence in which all thing "all things swerve. From their known course", or vanish like a dream, the church reminds man that his is not a "perishable home".

The sonnet "Composed in Roslin Chapel during a Storm" links the religious structures with the life of nature. The poet listens to the wind and marks the herbs growing in the now unused chapel among the sculptures:

That, green-grown,
Copy their beauty more and more, and preach,
Though mute, of all things blending into one.

Among the domestic structures, we may quote the pastor's home which is no cottage but represents an ideal state. With its pillared porch, mullioned windows and fretted cornice, the house set in the midst of flowers and shrubs and stately trees, has a "consummate harmony serene of gravity and elegance". The dignity and well-ordered proportions of the parsonage clearly symbolizes the harmony and rightness of the Pastor's life.

Wordsworth uses mainly three types of structures, ruined structure, domestic structure, religious structure. The domestic structures symbolize the life of man, but ruined and religious structures move between the poles of mutability and permanence.

Thus Wordsworth has made extensive use of symbols. Various aspects of landscape symbolizes various things, sounds tend to symbolize the unseen and spiritual; water symbolizes life, primarily that of feeling and thought, empire and permanence of soul. Structures are the symbol of the perishability of mortal power and glory.

References

1. Woolf, Virginia, "Playwrights or Playwriters", *The Hudson Review,* Autumn 1954, p. 470.
2. Marsh, Florence, *Wordsworth's Imagery: A Study in Poetic Vision,* Yale University Press, 1952, p. 36.
3. *Ibid.,* p. 57.
4. *Ivid.,* p. 93.

16

Humanism

Humanism as a way of life for the contemporary man has its devotees the entire world over and its sway over the intellectuals of the twentieth century is profound. Humanism emphasizes the dignity and worth of individual. Humanists' ideal expresses the dignity of man. Dr. P.T. Raju, an eminent Indian thinker, declares that "the present age is an age of humanism".[1] The history of humanism is long and involved. It continues to entertain several and diverse connotations. However, most humanists start with the dictum, "Man is the measure of all things"; certainly, but man as a rational being, not man as a bundle of particular sensations, subjective impressions, impulses, irrational prejudices, self will, mere eccentricities, oddities, foibles and fancies."[2] Whether we agree with this interpretation or not, but it is known that Greeks veered from theology and cosmology to man and thus it sowed the seed of humanism which was to grow sooner or later into a huge tree of myriad ramifications. Socrates' maxim "Know Thyself" forms an important tenet of humanism. Plato's humanism lies in his ethics. Aristotle regards reason as man's highest attribute and his glory. He says that man must be viewed as man, neither as angel nor as devil. There runs a strain of humanism through most classical Greek literature.

Renaissance humanism was an intellectual impulse. They believed that man was glorified in the classics, so they returned to the classical writings of great masters. Humanism has several devotees in the modern era too. Schiller popularized pragmatism as humanism. Naturalistic humanism has gained much popularity in the contemporary world. It holds that man is a wholly natural creature whose well-being rests on his own efforts unaided by transcendent support. Corliss Lamont, one of the chief exponents of naturalistic humanism, summarizes his viewpoint thus:

> *Humanism is the viewpoint that man has but one life to lead and should make most of it in terms of creative work and happiness; that human happiness is its own justification and requires no sanction or support from supernatural sources. . . . The Humanist philosophy persistently strives to remind men that their only home is the mundane world. There is no use of searching elsewhere for happiness and fulfilment, for there is no place else to go. We human beings must find our destiny and our promised land in the here and now, or not at all.*[3]

Religious humanism forms an important division of naturalistic humanism. Original Sin and human depravity is emphatically opposed by its adherents. They define God so strangely that He has been surreptitiously removed from the scene. The modern era has produced several other forms of humanism also. Now man is the sole agent of the further progress of evolution. Man is the central concern of humanism and its efforts are directed towards the recognition of the dignity of man as man. Its chief aim is the achievement of man's happiness, of course here and now.

Humanism in the Poetry of William Wordsworth

Wordsworth is the only poet who shows so great a reverence for man, as man. The French Revolution taught Wordsworth that every human being was intrinsically great and capable of infinite development. He began life with the most ardent hope for the moral regeneration of mankind but he had to renounce it reluctantly due to the excesses of French Revolution. But the poet set himself to examine the facts for himself. He would not give up his hopes for man till he had tested human nature in its elements. How was this to be done? "By stripping our own hearts naked, and by looking out of ourselves towards men who lead the simplest lives, and those most according to Nature, men who have never known false refinements, wayward and artificial desires, effeminate ways of thinking and feeling."[4] In his wanderings on the country roads he came in contact with the humblest human beings. Their strength and energy surprised him. He saw into the depths of human souls. He bowed in reverence:

To Nature and the power of human minds,
To men as they are men within themselves.

Nature never engrossed all thoughts of Wordsworth. Many were given to man, chiefly to the feelings of man. He aspired to become a philosophical poet, whose ultimate theme was not only Nature but also the heart of man. Wordsworth's temper was essentially democratic. He had lived in a democratic society; at Cambridge also he found a democratic atmosphere. As he says in *The Prelude,*

. . . we were brothers all
In honour as in one community,
Scholars and gentlemen.

He believed that the real secret of the unsatisfied passions and misery of mankind was deviation from living intercourse with Nature. He was confirmed when he found that in the remote dales of English Lake District human life attained a virtuous vision denied to the dwellers in great cities. His faith in mankind returned and man again became, "An object of delight of pure imagination and of love".

Wordsworth saw that man was at his best if set in his proper environment of Nature. He regarded him with genuine reverence. His panacea for the healing of his country was a return to nature. Lowliness and poverty cannot hide from him the great qualities of heart and character though these things are not seen by the selfish and unthinking. Human nature is a sacred thing to him. Even in its frailest and humblest form, he regards human nature with gentleness and sympathy. The real source of Wordsworth's reverence for man lies in his reverence for nature. He perceives that the rich are burdened with mean cares but the simple man, though he is under the stress of penury and labour, is noble and joyous as he lets nature lead him and exalt him. Wordsworth expresses this feeling in these lovely lines in the conclusion of the "Song at the Feast of Brougham Castle":

Love had he found in huts where poor men lie;
His daily teachers had been woods and rills,
The silence which is in the starry sky,
The sleep that is among the lonely hills.

Wordsworth sees man as a part of nature, experiencing joy and sorrow against the eternal background of nature. He does not work this out consciously as a philosophy by him as a philosophy but he feels it very strongly. He sees the resemblances between living man and nature. Some of his mighty men appear like the mighty oak trees of the ancient forests of England. Michael is one of such stout trees that grew in Grasmere Vale:

Upon the forest-side in Grasmere Vale
There dwelt a shepherd, Michael was his name;
An old man, stout of heart, and strong of limb.
His bodily frame had been from youth to age
Of an unusual strength; his mind was keen,
Intense, and frugal, apt for all affairs,
And in his shepherd's calling he was prompt
And watchful more than ordinary men.

In most of the poems of Wordsworth nature is the companion of man. The poet seems to love it for the sake of human association. In "Tintern Abbey" the poet is delighted to see the river Wye and the surrounding landscape not because all this is nature in general but because it is a particular part of nature, associated with man. He tells his sister:

Nor wilt thou then forget,
That after many wanderings, many years
Of absence, these steep woods and lofty cliffs,
And this green pastoral landscape, were to me
More dear, both for themselves and for thy sake!

Thus the colouring of imagination, which Wordsworth wanted to throw on natural objects, was nothing but this human association, which makes those, objects significant to the poet. Nature becomes transformed owing to its association with man. A man too old to ply a hatchet, a woman forsaken by her husband, an idiot sent at night to fetch a physician, a leech-gatherer bent double by age, a blind boy with a passion for adventure, a little girl who has lost her cloak, a ruined shepherd, a beggar, a pedlar, a thinker—these are the persons whom Wordsworth has celebrated in his poetry without condescension. These persons reveal the spirit of calm fortitude, dignity and sublimity in the midst of poverty and suffering.

The Prelude (Books VIII, IX, XIII) traces the growth of his love, sympathy and admiration for man and of his vision into the essential glory of man's personality—his life and character. Wordsworth's vision of man in his boyhood was deeply woven up with his love of Nature. Nature exalted his conception of man. He would often see the two in a vast frame of things melting into each other. The first vision of man in *The Prelude* (Book VIII) bears witness to this sense of harmony, when on a day of mist and fog, he saw the figure of a shepherd among the mountains. In this book, at several places, Wordsworth dwells upon the three vital reasons for his "first human love", his admiration, even reverence, for the primitive country-folk. The vision of man against nature's grandeur evokes in *The Prelude* some lofty lines where the poet feels a sudden "bursting forth of sympathy, inspiring and inspired", as he realizes "the vital pulse" of "one Being in all things" gaining its crowning manifestation in man.

. . . In the midst stood Man,
Outwardly, inwardly contemplated,
As, of all visible nature's crown, though born
Of dust, and kindred to the worm.

(*The Prelude* VIII, 485-88)

The man whom he "loved and reverenced" was even more exalted in his mind, conceived now as "a Spirit in time and space, and far diffused", He had faith in the glory of human spirit and in its endless promise. Wordsworth acknowledged the belief in the grandeur and the dignity of man. He regarded man not simply as a creature but retaining, god's image. In Wordsworth's lifetime this humanism had taken a colouring from Rousseau. The special nobility of man is therefore only to be looked for "in huts where poor men lie". From *The Borderers* to *The Excursion,* a sense of human spirit is communicated. The earliest long poem was *The Borderers. The Borderers* is precisely an attempt to present a similar crisis to that through which Wordsworth passed:

There was a plot,
A hideous plot against the soul of a man.
A man by pain and thought compelled to live,
Yet loathing life.
Suffering is permanent, obscure, and dark,
And shares the nature of infinity.
The mind of man, upturned,
Is in all natures a strange spectacle,
In some a hideous one.

Then there came the many noble poems "on man, on nature, and on human life". Political events in France, i.e., failure of French Revolution depressed Wordsworth, as he had some high hopes but it filled him with despair. When he came out of depression, he got a new vision. Let's see a statement of his new mood:

I found
Once more in Man an object of delight,
Of pure imagination, and of love;
And, as the horizon of my mind enlarged,
Again I took the intellectual eye
For my instructor, studious more to see
Great truths,

(*The Prelude* XIII, 48-54)

These lines show the essentially humanistic nature of Wordsworth's philosophy. He had his feet firmly on the common earth. It was his preference for human contacts, for "men as they are men within themselves", for living experience, which caused him to reject the philosophies which are based on false thoughts. He had perceived: "The utter hollowness of what we name the wealth of Nations". Long before Ruskin he had discovered that true wealth is lodged in

The dignity of individual Man,
Of man, no composition of the thought,
Abstraction, shadow, image, but the man
Of whom we read, the man whom we behold
With our own eyes.

(*The Prelude* XIII, 81-85)

This discovery bred in him
Enquire, said I, 'how much of mental power
And genuine virtue they possess who live
By bodily toil, labour exceeding far
Their due proportion, under all the weight
Of that injustice which upon ourselves
By composition of society
Ourselves entail.

(*The Prelude* XIII, 95-101)

Wordsworth therefore went out into the roads and into fields and cottages and resolved to dedicate himself to such man, ". . . my theme no other than the very heart of man". All these things clearly express the creed of humanism, that belief in the natural dignity of man, of which Wordsworth is perhaps the supreme exponent among the world's great poets. His so-called pantheism is also intimately connected with humanism, as he states:

And that the Genius of the Poet hence
May boldly take his way among mankind
Wherèver Nature leads; that he hath stood

By Nature's side among the men of old
And so shall stand for ever.

(*The Prelude* XIII, 295-299)

What Burns did for the Scotch peasant, Wordsworth has done for the shepherds and the husbandmen of England. He has done more than illustrate the virtues of a class. "Set amid the splendour and vivified by the influences of nature, he studied peasant life and attained a profound faith in man himself. Thus he attained a reverent understanding of the inherent grandeur of all human life."[5] Thus, Wordsworth's poetry was intensely aware of the humanity's afflicted will struggling in vain. He shaped the image of man repulsed by destiny and made it into everlasting nobility. This unique presentation we owe to Wordsworth and to Wordsworth alone.

References

1. Raju, P.T., *The Concept of Man* (ed.), S. Radhakrishnan and P.T. Raju, London, 1960, p. 15.
2. Stace, W.T., *A Critical History of Greek Philosophy*, London, 1962, p. 123.
3. Lamont, Corliss, *Humanism as a Philosophy*, New York, 1950, p. 21f.
4. *The Early Letters of William and Dorothy Wordsworth*, London, Oxford University Press, 1935, p. 295.
5. W.J. Dawson, The Makers of Modern English, p. 126.

Bibliography

Wordsworth

1. William Wordsworth, *A Guide through the District of the Lakes*, London: Longman & Co., Maxon and Whittaker & co. 1835.
2. Helen Darbishire (ed.), *Wordsworth's Poems in Two Volumes*, 1807.
3. Sir Ifor Evans (ed.), *Selections from Wordsworth*, Methuen &co. Ltd, 1935.
4. Thomas Hutchinson (ed.), *Wordsworth's Poetical Works*, Oxford University Press, 1910.
5. *The Early Letters of William and Dorothy Wordsworth*, Oxford University Press, London, 1935.
6. Ernest De Selincourt (ed.), *The Letters of William and Dorothy Wordsworth*, Vol. I , Oxford 1937-9.

Books on Wordsworth

1. Abbie Findlay Potts, *Wordsworth's Prelude: A Study of Its Form*, New York, Cornell University Press, 1953.

2. Carl Woodring, *Wordsworth,* Harvard University Press, 1968.

3. F.B.Pinion, *A Wordsworth Companion*, London, The Macmillan Press Ltd. 1984.

4. Florence Marsh, *Wordsworth's Imagery: A Study in Poetic Vision,* Yale University Press, 1952.

5. F.W, Batson, *Wordsworth—A Reinterpretation* Longmans, Green & Co. Ltd. London,1954.

6. F.W.H. Myers, *Wordsworth,* London, Macmillan & Co. Ltd.

7. Herbert Read, *Wordsworth,* Faber & Faber Ltd., London, 1949.

8. H.W. Garrod, *Wordsworth: Lectures and Essays,* London, Oxford University Press, 1923.

9. James, A.W. Heffernan, *Wordsworth's Theory of Poetry:The Transforming Imagination* New York Cornell University Press, 1969.

10. John Jones, *The Egotistical Sublime,* Chatto & Windus, 1954.

11. John F.Danby, *The Simple Wordsworth,* London: Routledge & Kegan Paul Ltd. 1960.

12. K.N.Khandelwal, *William Wordsworth: Selected Poems,* Agra, Laxmi Narain Agrawal, Educational Publishers.

13. Mary Moorman, *William Wordsworth—A Biography: The Early Years 1770-1803,* London: Oxford University Press, 1957.

14. Melvin Rader, *Wordsworth—A Philosophical Approach,* London, O.U.P., 1967.

15. Raghukul Tilak, *Wordsworth Select Poems,* Meerut, Rajhans Prakashan Mandir.

16. Raymond Dexter Havens, *The Mind of a Poet*, Baltimore, The Johns Hopkins Press, 1941.

17. S.B. Mukerji, *The Poetry of Wordsworth*, Vikas Publishing House Pvt. Ltd, New Delhi, 1976.

18. *The Ages of Wordsworth*, Preface to second Edition (ed.), C.H.H October (1897).

19. *Wordsworth: A Collection of Critical Essays* (ed.) M.H. Abrams: New Delhi, Prentice Hall of India Limited.

20. *Essays on Wordsworth: A Bi-Centenary Tribute* (ed.), Asloof Ahmed Ansari, Department of English A.M.U. Aligarh, 1973.

21. *Wordsworth : Lyrical Ballads* (ed.) Alun R. Jones and William Tydeman, London: Macmillan Press Ltd, 1972.

Contexts

1. Graham Hough, *The Romantic Poets*, Hutchinson's University Library, London, 1953.

2. J.R. Watson, *English Poetry of the Romantic Period*, 1789-1830, Essex Longman Group Limited.

3. M.H. Abrams, (ed.) *English Romantic Poets*, London, Oxford University Press, 1960.

4. Ram Bilas Sharma, *Studies in Nineteenth Century English Poetry*, Pustak Bhawan, Agra 1961.

5. W.J. Dawson: *The Makers of Modern English*, Meerut, Shalabh Book House, 1985.

Articles

1. Alun R. Jones, *'The Compassionate World' English*, Volume XIX Spring 1970, Number 103.

2. Harold Bloom, *"The Myth of Memory and Natural Man"* Quoted in M.H. Abrams (ed.), *English Romantic Poets*, London, Oxford University Press, 1960.

3. Leavis, "Wordsworth", in *Revaluation: Tradition and Development in English poetry.*

4. Lionel Trilling, "The Immortality ode," in *The Liberal Imagination; Essays in Literature and Society,* New York, Viking Press, 1950.

5. Masoodul Hasan, *'Mystical Elements in Wordsworth's Poetry' Essays on Wordsworth: A Bi-Centenary Tribute* (ed.), Asloof Ahmed Ansari, Department of English A.M.U. Aligarh, 1973.

6. Neil Hertz, *"Wordsworth and The Tears of Adam"*, Quoted in M.H.Abrams (ed.), *English Romantic Poets,* London, Oxford University Press, 1960.

7. Roger Sharrock, *'The Prelude: the Poet's Journey to the Interior', English,* Volume XIX Spring 1970, number 103.

Index